NO ACTING PLEASE

ERIC MORRIS AND JOAN HOTCHKIS

A WHITEHOUSE/SPELLING PUBLICATION

FIRST EDITION

Cover Art By Paul Whitehouse

Photos by Ronald Magid

LIBRARY OF CONGRESS
CATALOG CARD NUMBER
76-49366

ACKNOWLEDGEMENTS

We wish to thank John Fiorito, student and associate, for the endless hours of taped class sessions that were invaluable in the writing of this book, and for his involvement and support.

And to Paul Whitehouse for his insight and encouragement in the publication of "No Acting Please".

With gratitude to Daniel Spelling for the tireless efforts put forth in editing the text. For him it was truly a "labor of love".

And to all the actors that were instrumental in the evolvement of the techniques herein.

Eric Morris
Joan Hotchkis

My special thanks and love to Joy King for the support, love, and encouragement she gave me all along the way.

Eric

A Whitehouse/Spelling Publication

I

FOREWORD

Eric and I met as students in the sense memory class he describes in this book. No one was more zealous in pursuit of "the work" than "the manic-depressive dane". Nothing daunted Morris. Not the actress who really fainted in "Dark Of The Moon"; not the actor who wore rubber bands and couldn't figure out which side of his mouth to spit his Ludens cough drops; not me as the nazi of your dreams driving him quivering and vulnerable through the concentration camp of his; not even being called the most pretentious ass this side of Sasha Guitry at four a.m. by some angry young actor with Gallo on his lips. Eric was always helpful to others, and most important to himself.

The reality is no one can tell you how to act. My own feelings and observations tell me it requires deep personal commitment to allow any individual to move from that vague desirous state of "I'm gonna be an actress (or actor)" to a point where the actor has some vague sense that every part in which they are cast is not some incredible piece of luck like saying the secret word on "You Bet Your Life", but the result of some solidy acquired skills which, in there, where the truth is, he can call his own.

No book is going to contain all of the things which have helped other actors arrive at a free use of their talent.

As is pointed out in this book, many people feel any academic approach to acting is in conflict with the "Gypsy", or intuitive element of this craft. I suppose the reason Eric asked me to write something for the front of his book is because we have been in many classes, workshops, groups, whatever, together where we observed an experienced talent struggling for agonizing, tedious, and hysterical periods of time to break through and become expressive. If you're interested in this sort of thing, it can be an inspiring process. It's not for everyone. It's not "entertaining", though it can be. There are no guarantees or diplomas, but it can be deeply satisfying to acquire and be a part of anothers acquisition of the tools which allow them to enjoy and express their talent.

The concept of "Being" as opposed to "Acting" is Eric's focus here. Along the way he describes exercises related to, actor's adversary number one, Tension, relating, stimuli, levels of consciousness, behavior, vulnerability, unpredictability, specificty, and many others. What is described has worked in some way for one actor or another. The Method is, "If it works, use it".

— *JACK NICHOLSON*

TABLE OF CONTENTS

I

BEING

On Being

Acting is the art of creating genuine realities on a stage. No matter what the material,
the actor's fundamental question is: "What
is the reality and how can I make it real to
me?" In this kind of training the actor dis-
covers himself fully both on the stage and
off, since the exercises in this book repeatedly demand an integration of living
and acting. It is a way of life, not just
a way of work.

For the first few years I taught acting to
the letter. I was faithful to the Stanis-
lavsky-derived techniques I had learned and
my approach to creating realities on the
stage encompassed in sense memory, affective
memory, task choices, etc. Over this period
I became increasingly aware that some actors
could use the work quite well and other actors, also talented, couldn't make it happen.
It didn't work for them. Even for the actors
that did it well, there remained huge areas
unreachable to them and their work often
seemed clinical and academic. I became frustrated. I began to doubt "the Method" as a
total approach, began to believe the pessi-
mistic sayings of the master acting teachers,
that only two per cent of actors could use
"the Method". And even in my own work as an
actor I was frustrated, disappointed in the
results I was getting. It was about this
time that I started asking some questions,
such as how can the same technique work for

1

everybody. Not everybody is the same. We all
have different fears, different inhibitions, a
variety of different concerns and certainly
different backgrounds. Why are actors afraid
to talk about themselves personally? Why do
acting teachers shy away from discussing the
personal elements in acting? Why is everybody
so secretive?

I came to the realization that while there's
lip service paid to using your personal life
on stage and getting "deep" into your own emotions, few actors have the courage to do this
and most teachers aren't even aware of the necessity for this kind of search. You can't
teach a man to run if he hasn't got legs. Nor
can you teach a person to act if he isn't connected to his inner self. I started to develop
an approach to acting which embarked on a
search of the self and led toward usage of the
self on stage. Out of this approach came a
whole system of work which included some of
the skills of "The Method", but these skills
now became really applicable because they were
emanating from a really personal nucleus. I
discovered that one of the reasons why many
actors couldn't use the Stanislavsky system
was because of the separation between technique and personal reality. How can a system
designed to be personal work for actors who
are not personal and don't even know what they
feel?

I invented exercises which required that actors
search for their own personal points of view
about everything and express it. Hundreds of
exercises evolved out of working with actors
who were struggling with individual problems.
Some of these exercises are named after the
actors they were first designed for, although
later, of course, they applied to other actors.
The "rounds" were born. I demanded that actors

2

encounter each other in Reluctancy Exercises, in Honesty Stream of Consciousness, in Ego Reconstructions and other "round" exercises. (We'll describe all of these later.) I encouraged them to be extremely personal with each other, to do away with their social impositional life and to experience the real moment no matter what the imagined consequences.

At first it was unsettling. People offended each other. People walked out of class, broke down and cried, became hysterical. But something important started to happen to these actors that had never happened in their work before. A kind of visceral reality superseded their concerns about how they looked, how they sounded, or how the scene "should go". I started to see the real people in the scenes, as they were when they weren't acting. People were beginning to BE, at first only in brief moments here and there, but the difference between BEING and acting was glaringly obvious to all of us. Once the actors had tasted these moments of BEING, their appetites were whetted for more. Both actors and audience became dissatisfied with less than the truth.

In my classes I urged each actor to do the most difficult thing first, because then all the less difficult problems were done away with in one fell swoop. For example, a girl would come into class very uptight, very proper, possibly with parochial school background, wanting desperately to act, but paralyzed with her concern about being a nice girl. The first exercise I'd give her might be a Vulgarity or perhaps a Sensuality or an Anti-Social. If it was a Vulgarity, I'd ask her to stand up in front of the class

3

and be crude, vile, pick her nose, scratch
her ears, belch, use profanity, put her hand
on her crotch. All of these things would be
overwhelmingly difficult for her to do. But
even if she should do part of these, the ice
was cracked. The class would accept and encourage her and the atmosphere was permissive,
supporting her awareness that she has the
right to do these things and it's okay. After
this one exercise, the actress might be freed
of a whole cluster of social mannerisms which
had stood between her and her real feelings.

The results of these Therapy Exercises were
amazing. What in my first five years of teaching had remained a persistent problem with the
student was now alleviated immediately and in
several months didn't exist. The solving of
problems like this allowed us to get deeper
into the rich life which lay beneath. In the
process of discovering themselves, the actors
became aware of not only how they felt on a
moment-to-moment basis here and now, but also
of the scores of things that had affected them
throughout their lives. Now we were no longer
just using sensory choices that sounded good
and usable in a scene. The sensory choices
had become more personal and private and affecting. We were beginning to touch the
nucleus of the individual self. A more personal and exciting reality began to exist on
the stage in the framework of a scene, not
consistently at first, but with continued
work, more and more. Often in class I would
give an actor a "Jellybean" which is a statement, a thought, or a concept designed to
pin-point specifics, or inspire the actor to
think in a certain area of craft or personal
concern. Sometimes a simple three word
"Jellybean" would take the place of a long-
winded critique, and zero in on the overview
of the entire problem.

4

JELLYBEAN: NO ACTING, PLEASE

I must define at this point what I mean by BEING. It is not a word I chose accidentally. It came to me from working with actors who were trying to achieve that state of life on stage which was the fullest, the most real and the most total. This state usually occurred when they would get closest to what they really felt, and farthest from their customary "acting". When they were closest to what they really felt, their behavior on stage included all kinds of life, infinite colors, distractions, interruptions and unpredictable changes of emotions. Even the identifiable emotions - anger, hate, love, fear - had more facets when they came out of this kind of reality. When an actor in a scene attempts to achieve a particular emotion, what usually occurs is that his presentation of that emotion is flat and one-dimensional. I refer to this phenomenon as "on the nose" acting. It happens because the actor is concerned with delivering the result "on the nose", so consequently the emotion doesn't contain all the elements from which it came, the sources, the impetus which caused the emotion in the first place. When the actor is functioning from a BEING state, all that he feels is included in the life being expressed, and then the resulting emotion contains all of his own personal truth and reality.

When commenting upon an actor's work, telling him or her it was fuller and more believable, I'd invariably get the response, "But Eric, I didn't do anything! I was just being me! What about the theatrical demands?" Ironically, when the actor would approach the BEING state. he'd become much more theatrical and he'd meet the demands of his material on a more complex and imaginative level, because more kinds of life, more subtleties of reality were going on. The exciting thing about successfully achieving BEING on stage or in front of the camera is that it stands out like a beacon in the night. The actor brings to his work the undeniable uniqueness of himself and the work takes on a personal quality that has a fabric incomparable to anyone or anything else. It is unpredictable to the actor. It is filled with inspiration and surprises which eliminate conventional expectations. It has a crisp "one time" feeling that actually makes the audience believe it is happening here and now for the very first time, because, in a sense, it really is.

The craft is not designed to be an esoteric laboratory involvement, but an applicable approach to achieving the most exciting life possible. In the last analysis, if it doesn't produce results, it is only good sounding philosophy.

BEING is a state you work to achieve. To BE you must find out what you feel and express it totally. Let one impulse lead to another without intellectual editing, including all the life that is going on - the interruptions, interferences, and distractions. These elements should all be included in the behavior. *Do no more or less than you feel.* BEING is the only place from which you can create organic reality.

Taped Excerpt From BEING Exercise

The scene: A class for professional actors at the Eric Morris Acting Workshop in Hollywood. Everyone is seated in the theatre seats. The stage is bare except for a chair in the center.

Eric says, "E.J., get up there." E.J. walks
on stage. She is a musical comedy actress
known for her soubrette-ingenue roles on
stage and television. The following dialogue
was taken from a tape of the class session.

Eric: Alright. I want you to sit in the
        center of the stage and BE. Do no
        more or less that what you feel.

E.J. sits down on the chair and begins to
pull herself together. She sits up straight,
smiles winningly at the audience, folds her
hands in her lap. She is getting ready to
present the best part of herself to the world.

Eric: What are you doing?

E.J.:   What do you mean, what am I doing?

Eric: How do you feel?

E.J.:   What do you mean, how do I feel?

Eric: You're doing things on stage that have
        nothing to do with what is.

E.J.:   Well, I'm nervous. I feel a little
        shaky. You've got me upset.

Eric: Okay.

E.J.   I don't like to be picked on.

Eric: You're not being picked on.

E.J.:   The hell I'm not. I know what you're
        doing.

Eric: Okay. I think you're angry and I think
        you're surpressing it and functioning
        in spite of it. You're hostile and

7

defensive and you're functioning above
that.

E.J.: Yes, I am.

Eric: That's not BEING. That's not BEING at
all. That's "I'm BEING in spite of myself." What's that? That's not BEING.

E.J.: Well, I don't know what the hell you
want me to do, Eric! You told me to
sit here and I'm trying to sit here!

Eric: Okay. Do you want to cry now?

E.J.: (Starting to cry) No!

Eric: It's not pure.

E.J.: (Sobbing) Stop it!

Eric: Stop what?

E.J.: (Sobbing and screaming) I felt so great
coming into this lousy class!

Eric: You do this, one, to avoid finding out
what's going on and two, to get yourself off the spot and three, to get out
of dealing with what you have to deal
with. You still aren't being. You're
closer because you've expurgated a
little shit. How do you feel?

E.J.: I feel great. Thanks. I really do. I
mean I'm so tired. I worked all day, I
earned - earned a lot of money this week
and I'm tired. I didn't even want to
come tonight, but I did. Because I love
to come here and be spit upon!

Eric: Is that what you think we're doing?

E.J. doing BEING exercise.

E.J.:   No, I'm teasing. I know what you're
        doing Eric. . . Somewhere. I don't
        know. . . (crying a little). And
        BEING - I mean - just BEING - I'm
        trying to figure it out.

John (a student): You can't figure it out.

Eric: Maybe you shouldn't try to figure it
        out. Maybe you should just find out
        how you feel. So far you've told us
        what you did this week and about com-
        ing here tonight -

E.J.:   (Yelling) Well, I felt alright, Eric,
        before I got here!

Eric: What makes you think that you don't
        feel alright now? Because -

E.J.:   Because I don't!

Eric: Does alright mean this as opposed to
        that? What does alright mean?

E.J.:   It means alright.

Eric: Alright means everything. You're still
        not doing the exercise. You're avoid-
        ing and evading, evading and avoiding.
        You know how you get to BE? You get
        to "How do I feel now and am I func-
        tioning in terms of how I feel now?
        If not, why not and what can I do to
        get to that?"

E.J.:   My hands are shaking.

Eric: You took your glasses off. You keep
        maintaining that you can't see and
        then you take your glasses off so that
        you won't see.

E.J.:   (Laughs)

Eric: Does that protect you?

E.J.:   Will you wait until I finish wiping my
        eyes, okay?

E.J. puts her glasses on and looks out at the
audience.

Eric: How do you feel?

E.J.:   Nervous.

Eric: Okay. Let's see it.

E.J.:   I don't know what do do!

Eric: Admit it.

E.J.:   I just did!

Eric: Where are you nervous?

E.J.:   My hands are shaking.   (She holds them
        in her lap.)

Eric: Let us see that. Share that. How can
        you BE if you want to hide? You're
        looking at the floor now. Now that
        you've got your glasses on and can see,
        you don't want to see. You know why?
        Because you want to avoid the responsi-
        bility of feeling the feedback. Deal
        with the feedback.

E.J.:   You mean the looks I'm getting from the
        people?

Eric: And the involvement in the people and
        the moment to moment changes and every-
        thing.

E.J.: Everything. . . and say what I see coming out of them, right?

Eric: Just BE. Feel what you feel, communicate what you feel, experience what you feel, allow what you feel.

E.J.: (Starts to cry) I'm looking at Morty and I feel like crying.

Eric: Why do you feel the responsibility to explain that to us? If you feel like crying, cry! Look at Morty and cry! Don't tell me about it. That isn't BEING.

E.J.: (Sobs louder)

Eric: Why are you crying now, because I'm yelling at you?

E.J.: No. No, it's not because you're yelling at me.

Eric: What is it?

E.J.: (Sobs and says something incoherent)

Eric: Okay. Let it run its course. Don't cover your mouth. That's not BEING. Let it run its course and maybe it'll give way to something else. Don't cut it off. Let it happen. Let it run its way out.

E.J.: (Sobs even louder with prolonged moans)

Eric: You know, I don't believe you. You're doing everything except what I'm asking you to do. Almost all of your hostility and defensiveness and all of your crying is something which is self-stimulated, something that you encourage to happen.

E.J.: Oh, fuck, Eric! I felt so great when I walked in that door tonight!

Eric: Now wait a minute, wait a minute. Let's iron out what you mean by I felt so great. Do you mean now you feel terrible?

E.J.: (Sobbing) Well, I really feel shaky.

Eric: As opposed to what? . . . Listen to me.

E.J.: I am, Eric!

Eric: Why do you feel the necessity to be defensive? I'm not attacking you. I'm trying to help you.

E.J.: I know you are.

Eric: Do you believe that?

E.J.: Yeah, I do.

Eric: Okay, fine. I think that you function on a level which is above BEING. Beyond BEING. It is a level of social obligation. I think you are enormously affected by social obligation. Therefore, when social obligation is heightened by the presence of people and the obligation to see and be seen, you feel the necessity to do. And when that is frustrated, the only thing you then can do is to cry, to feel upset and frustrated and anxiety-ridden. And that expresses itself in a single way - the way you saw it tonight. But your expression isn't pure. It comes out of frustration and instead of being frustrated

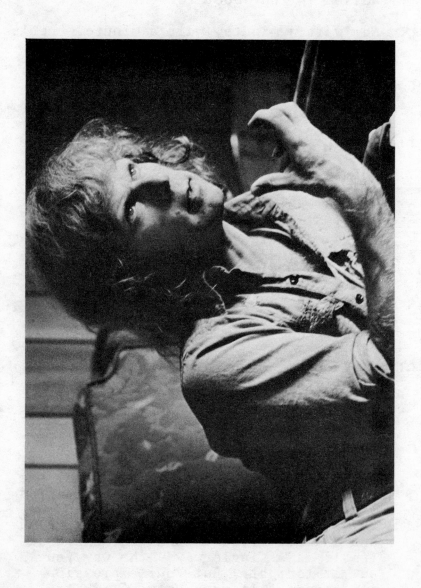

Eric directing BEING exercise.

15

and expressing that, you go to the
crying and yelling because that ex-
purgates the tension, the anxiety of
being on the spot. It alleviates
your confusion and it fulfills an
element which is very important to
you: meeting the social obligation.
You have been doing what you think
people expect of you for so long that
you don't know what you expect of
yourself or how to get it. When the
social obligation is a big question
mark, as it is to you in this exercise, you function on a level which
you think is interesting - theatrically
attractive. You function on a level
of life which feels more secure to you
than stopping that indulgence and
finding out what the component parts
of E.J. are. Now I interrupted you
constantly for one very important reason: I wanted you to know from the
outset what you do and what you don't
do to find out what you feel, who you
are and what's going on here and now.
Every single time I pinned you, you
responded the same way - crying or
defensive yelling, instead of really
allowing yourself to be hurt, openly
confused, afraid, helpless, whatever -
and allowing those impulses to express
themselves moment to moment. Do you
know what I mean by BEING?

E.J.: I do now.

Eric: Okay. BEING is "I'm sitting here, I'm
looking around the room, I feel boring
and dull and that's okay. I'm crossing
my legs. I'm beginning to feel a little
self-conscious. All these people are
looking at me."

17

E.J.: You mean BEING is like a stream of con-
       sciousness?

Eric: It can be. It can be anything that is.
       I'm just doing this out loud to demon-
       strate, but you don't have to do it out
       loud. You don't have to open your mouth
       unless you're impelled to. (Continuing
       the demonstration) "I feel a little
       tension creeping into my neck. Hello,
       tension. I know you're there. Every-
       body's looking at me expectantly and I
       feel like I should do something. That
       lump in my stomach tells me to do some-
       thing quick. But I don't have to do
       anything." That's BEING. Whatever is,
       is. Alright, how do you feel?

E.J.: Confused. Totally confused.

Eric: Good. I see that.

E.J.: What's good about being confused? The
       way I feel right now I couldn't say
       three lines in any script.

Eric: That's okay. For right now. But you're
       better off now instrumentally than when
       you got on the stage.

E.J.: What's that supposed to mean?

Eric: Alright, let me be a little presumptuous
       E.J., and say that had I given you a
       piece of material when you first walked
       up on the stage, you would have read it
       well. But this is not a reading class.
       I am convinced I would have been able
       to predict every movement, every sound,
       every expression you made. However, if
       you were to continue the life that's
       going on now in you and include it into

18

that piece of material, I'm sure I wouldn't be able to begin to predict or anticipate what you would do.

John: Yeah, but Eric, if she went with the life that is right now in her and the obligation of the material was to be confident, maybe, secure, demure, the perfect hostess, wouldn't the existing life be wrong for the material?

Eric: Sure. But that's the point at which you begin. That doesn't mean that the life she's experiencing is right for the material, but from this state of confusion, she can work for a choice stimulating the reality that would make her feel the way she wants to feel for the material. This confusion, this anxiety she's feeling, is the bedrock here-and-now reality. It can be changed to another kind of here-and-now reality, whereas the state she assumes is an unaffectable state.

E.J.: Oh! So this is just getting ready? Preparation?

Eric: Exactly. Acting is almost all getting ready, because if you're ready and prepared to act, then you can.

BEING Exercise Critique

JELLYBEAN: BEFORE ACTING MUST COME BEING

The BEING Exercise you have just read, whether the actor does it by himself or in a group, is different each time because each actor's true state of BEING and the things he does to avoid

19

BEING are unique. The success of the exercise as demonstrated by E.J. and me depends on the skill and experience of the teacher or director. The BEING Exercise could become a mind-manipulating weapon in the hands of a teacher or director who does not fully understand the work and who has not himself experienced it. I take responsibility for manipulating E.J., second-guessing her and leading her into certain areas because, after fifteen years of teaching experience, I am able to ascertain the difference between creative manipulation and destructive manipulation. The motives of the teacher and his perception of knowing *what* to say and *when* are crucial factors and make all the difference.

The craft of acting is the art of BEING and there are many techniques and literally hundreds of exercises to help you accomplish this state of BEING. We hope that in the following chapters you will be able to learn and use these exercises and include them in your own approach. It's not something that happens overnight. You have to practice daily. You have to find a system that works for you. That happens by experimentation, by looking around, going to different teachers, and testing the techniques for yourself.

Most actors learn to act by imitating other actors. By the time you've had fifteen or twenty years of watching actors on a screen or stage, you've acquired a whole unconscious repertoire of mannerisms and things to do. We usually emulate those we admire, but this kind of emulation is dangerous for actors, because you end up externally doing things that come from other actors and these imitations rob you of finding out who you are and what you have to contribute. You're as individual as your fingerprints and indivi-

20

duality is what you have to contribute. You
are not only the best thing you have, you're
the only thing you have.

Unfortunately, among actors and actresses,
there's a stigma against hard work. Many
cling to the myth that they can get by on
their talent alone without knowing their
craft - the delusion of theatrical immortal-
ity. Others believe that to study a craft
will actually spoil their talent by inter-
fering with "natural instincts". Others
depend precariously on rabbits' feet, making
the sign of the cross before going on stage,
never whistling in the dressing room, vitamin
B-12 shots, honey and hot lemon juice, uppers,
downers, and grass. Some of these things
make you feel good, but none of them help
you to act.

An actor must take a stance somewhere. He
must decide at what level of creativity he
wants to function and then use his time at
the cost of success for awhile, if need be,
and in the face of ridicule. He must find
and apply a craft until he makes it a habit,
and a very dependable one. Most of the
exercises have become vital techniques for
acting therapy. Acting problems are often
life problems. If you have difficulty exposing some aspect of yourself offstage,
you'll have even greater difficulty exposing
it on stage. Often an acting problem cannot
be solved without changing something in the
actor's life.

People come into the profession of acting crip-
pled by all the taboos of our society, rules
made by parents, schools and churches. All of
these restrictions are anti-BEING: "Children
should be seen and not heard. . . Don't talk
back. . . Stop daydreaming, you're wasting

time. . . Be nice. . . Men don't cry. . . Nice
girls don't do that. . ." And thousands of
other instructions which insidiously corrode
your freedom. As an actor you must spend the
bulk of your time in the training process finding and freeing yourself.

What stops us from BEING? Consequences. Fear
of ridicule. Rejection. Violation of our
"image". Longevity and position ("I've been
acting so long I should be able to do more than
I'm doing right now, so I have to promote the
image that I'm better off than I am.") Age
("I'm too old for this experimental stuff.")
Fear of failure. Judgement. All these things
and many more are obstacles to BEING.

Loosely defined, talent is the ability to be
affected by an enormous number of things and
to express imaginatively the fullness of everything you feel. But because of social pressures, we as actors have learned to accept only
the positive elements of our talent and deny
the negative elements. And you must not do
that. As a creative instrument you cannot say,
"This is okay and it's alright for me to feel
that and expose that, but this other thing is
not okay and it's not alright for me to expose
that." You can't do this because what happens
is that you short-circuit your instrument. If
you sit there and say to yourself, "I'm not
going to show anybody what's going on underneath.", you've put a capper on everything you
do. One expression leads to another and the
minute you stop any one impulse, the flow of
your BEING stops. Most people fail at the
opening gun. I can tell if an actor is functioning in ten seconds, as soon as he gets up
from where he's sitting. One can see either
the inclusion of what's going on or the suppression of it, either the presence of life
or the absence of life. Most actors are in

trouble the moment they begin. The whole concept of BEING - BEING BEFORE DOING - BEING
BEFORE ACTING - is based on the acknowledge-
ment, the acceptance and the expression of
everything you feel.

Most people think of emotions as negative or
positive. They place a value judgement on
"nice" or "not nice" emotions, "bad" feelings
and "good" feelings. But I don't believe
there is anything negative or positive about
what you feel. As we often say in class
"Everything's a Number Six." I arbitrarily
chose the number six, it could be a number
eight. The point of choosing any number is
to say that all emotions have equal value
and no singular emotional response has more
value than the last. At auditions most actors choose highly volatile material through
which to demonstrate their wares. Very few
actors decide on simple scenes. The reason
for this is the misconception that the stronger emotions are more important. I'm a sensitive, vulnerable, highly volatile human
being. Those are the positive elements of
my talent. The same things that make me
sensitive and vulnerable and volatile also
make me insecure, anxious, depressed, tense
and hostile. The same elements that affect
me positively also affect me negatively.
So I come into the producer's office. He's
casting a film. Do I say to him, "I'm a
sensitive, vulnerable, volatile instrument,
but I'm also depressed, insecure, and anxious."? No, I can't say that to him. I
don't want him to see my depression and fear.
So I hide it. And the minute I hide something, suppress anything, I hide it all.
And then I'm not functioning.

So what do I do instead? I walk in and sit
down and instead of getting into Gee-what-

great-weather-we're-having-and-how-heavy-the-
traffic-was-coming-in-from-the-Valley, the
producer says to me, "How are you?" And I
might say, "Well. . . not so good at this
moment. I feel a little tense, because I
haven't worked in a long time and I'd like
to get this job and I'm afraid to even tell
you that because you might think I'm too
insecure to do it, even if you hired me.
Except that to really show you who I am, so
you can see my talent, I have to start from
how I'm feeling at this moment."

Using this approach, you might alienate fifty
per cent of your prospective employers. But
the other fifty per cent, the lovers of truth,
will respond to you because out of the usually
phony interview you will have created a meaningful moment. In this sense, the cripples
might really be the long distance runners.
If you expose your limitations and let people
see them, you no longer have anything to hide.
You're functioning on a level of reality and
from a level of reality, you can be creative.
From a level of phony bullshit you cannot
create anything. Once you've established
your state of BEING and you're functioning
in terms of what is, you are now ready to
deal with the author's intent and the obligations of the material. You will find and
execute a choice to bring you to the state
of life that the material demands. In other
words, you go from your existing state of
BEING to that state of BEING required by the
material.

JELLYBEAN:
IF YOU START WITH AN EMPTY BLACKBOARD,
YOU CAN WRITE ANYTHING ON IT

From Joan's Journal, 1970:

First Contact with BEING

I'd studied several years with two of the
finest acting teachers in the country, San-
ford Meisner and Lee Strasberg. I was a
hardworking student, dedicated to the method
I was being taught. Sandy and Lee teach
quite differently, but they shared in common
a belief that it wasn't sound professional
training to expose your personal choices to
the class or talk about your personal life.
They kept saying things like, "Don't tell us
about that. That's too personal. . . You
must try not to be so anxious. . . Don't tell
us your choice. It will dissipate it for
you." For years my work was stuck on an
academic level. It was labored and impersonal and all the techniques showed.

When I first came into Eric's classes, I was
repelled by the lack of privacy - actors
talking about their mothers and fathers in
intimate detail, weeping or howling with
glee or smashing the air with their fists -
actors sitting around in a circle while each
one tells the thing he is most reluctant to
reveal - actors cradling each other like
babies, crooning lullabies. It looked like
an insane asylum to me. I was terrified. I
thought if I gave away my secrets, threw them
into the public pot, my few treasures would
be lost forever and then my acting would be
even emptier and drier than it was. But Eric
kept saying, "That's mystical bullshit. What
are you, a one-choice actress? A three-choice
actress? Your life is full of experiences!
You're rich with choices!"

I knew down to my bones I'd find the missing
link in this kind of training. And I did.
And soon. I found the connection to myself.
All those personal feelings and fantasies
which had been locked out of my work began
to flood in. The few choices I'd been using
again and again multiplied - miraculously
bloomed into countless others. The techniques
I'd learned before - improvisation, sense memory, personalization, affective memory - were
made much more specific and personal so that I
could really depend on them to ignite my work.
and, paradoxically, the more skilled I've become, the less the skill shows, which proves
that what Eric often says, "The craft is designed to do away with itself."

BEING in Relation to Scene Work

JELLYBEAN: THE UNCONSCIOUS IS WHERE
YOUR TALENT LIVES

The scene: The Professional Class at the Eric
Morris Actor's Workshop. Connie and Danny
have just finished a scene. They've explained
what they were working for and now they're
waiting for the critique. Connie is an experienced actress in her early forties, doing
her first scene in class tonight. Danny is
an attractive young actor, a student in the
class for two and one half years. At the moment he is agitated and dissatisfied with his
work.

Eric : How do you feel, Connie?

Connie: I feel okay.

Eric : How do you feel, Danny?

Danny : Oh God, Eric, I feel constipated.

26

Eric   : That's okay. (Turns to class sitting
          in the theatre.) Alright, what would
          anybody like to say?

(Comments from the actors lasted about a half
hour. For the most part they were supportive
and critically constructive. Part of each
actor's growth depends on his ability to perceive and articulate the processes of work.)

John   : Well, it was a pretty good first
          scene. I mean, you know, it's not
          easy to get up there and do a first
          scene. I'm talking about Connie
          now. What I really feel about her
          work, Eric, is that it was too
          general. (Class protocol requires
          that you talk to the actor through
          Eric. Direct criticism often pro-
          vokes two-way conversations which
          can lead to defensiveness and then
          the points are lost.) She said she
          "personalized" her sister, but I
          didn't see that. How did she work
          for that? She said she had an
          "intention" of seducing Danny, but
          as far as I could tell, she was too
          self-involved to even see him. I
          didn't see any relationship between
          them at all. And her lines - uh -
          they just sounded like lines, not
          like talk. As for Danny, I liked
          a lot of what he did. I think
          Danny has a tendency to make trouble
          for himself. He comments on what
          he's doing instead of allowing it
          just to be. He's too hard on him-
          self. But I must say I see more and
          more of Danny everytime he does a
          scene here

Savannah: I don't altogether agree with John

27

about Connie. I mean, my God, I saw
such wonderful underlying sensitivity. I don't want Connie to leave
here tonight without knowing how
special I feel she is. I saw moments of real need and loneliness
that - well - she really touched me.
I agree with John that she has to
learn to work with choices specifically, but let us see more of
Connie in the work. Connie, you're
beautiful. And Danny, will you for
Christ's sake let yourself alone?
All this self-beating. I mean, I
really get tired of it. You don't
need to do that anymore, Danny.
It's all there. . .

(About fourteen other people commented, and
then Eric gave his critique.)

Eric : Connie, I know exactly how you work
from watching the scene. I know
that's pompous to say. I haven't
seen everything you've done, but I
know how you work. Now, it took
you 'X' number of years to get as
good as you are with what you do.
Isn't that true? Would you accept
that?

Connie: Yes, I've done a lot of work.

Eric : I can see that. And it's not bad
work. It's good. I mean, if somebody walked in off the street and
saw you do that scene, they wouldn't
say that was bad work. They wouldn't
say that girl can't act. Nobody in
his right mind would say that. It
wasn't great work, but it certainly
wasn't bad work. It represented a

28

kind of training and background and it was
certainly professional. And it took 'X'
number of years to get to that. So if you
take 'X' number of years and you say "Okay,
I'm going to learn Stanislavsky, Strasberg,
Uta Hagen, Eric Morris, Stella Adler, whatever. I'm going to learn that technique."
A equals B equals C equals D. All of that
is a fixed process insofar as it is a language. But none of it means anything to
anybody unless you have a canvas to paint
it on. I can come in here and say, "I've
just invented the greatest oil colors known
to man. Nobody's ever had these colors!"
But what do you put them on? You gotta
have a canvas. The canvas is you. Your
canvas is BEING. Now had you done something else in 'X' number of years, you'd be
behaving differently here tonight. If ninety per cent of your time went into BEING
and learning how to BE, finding out who you
are and what makes you function, and ten
per cent went into your "system", your technique or whatever you call it, that would be
a proper proportion. The craft of acting
can be taught to an idiot in six months.
It's not hard. It's very easy. It makes a
lot of sense. What's difficult, what gets
in the way are the obstacles to BEING, which
are your obligations - theatrical, social
and emotional. All your obligations get in
your way. That's why we have exercises like
I Allow, I Permit, I Accept, Personal Inventory, and Double Exposure. The main thing
is not an acting problem. It's a living
problem. What you can't allow yourself to
feel out there, you won't allow yourself to
feel here on stage. You can't make a separation between life out there and life on
stage. You can't walk out of her tonight
and think that you're dealing with an acting
problem. You're dealing with a living

problem. There isn't anything you cannot do
on the stage. You might be wrong. You might
go out in left field, and even throw the play,
which isn't what I'm recommending. But I
would love to go to the theatre and take the
chance of having an actor throw the play because of his courage, his risk-taking, than to
see a predictable, staid, conventional performance. I'd like to go see Tennessee Williams
and have the second act suddenly be Arthur
Miller. That's better than seeing how everybody "does" Tennessee Williams.

You don't work for a choice in parallel to
doing the scene, Connie, which is what you
were attempting here. Working for a choice is
a process where you ask sensory questions and
you let your senses answer and you commit
yourself to that process totally even at the
cost of the scene until that process bears
some kind of behavioral fruit. Then if your
behavior is not what you want for the scene,
you adjust your choice or find a different
choice. You always include everything that
is going on. *There is no acting in acting.*
When you're acting, you're not BEING. I know
as sure as I'm sitting in this chair, Connie,
that what you want will happen for you, if you
do this kind of work.

Danny, I agree with a lot of the comments
about your making trouble for yourself. I
could see that you were in trouble. I could
see that a lot of your behavior on the stage
came out of frustration at not being able to
free the things you felt. It's okay to have
problems, if the life comes out of them. But
I want to talk about walking the fence. You
walked the fence between what you felt and
what you thought should be there in the scene.
You partially included the life that was going
on in you and because of that partial inclusion

30

I found you interesting, sometimes compelling
and unpredictable. But instead of surrender-
ing yourself to all of your problems and letting the words come totally out of that life,
you kept commenting on your inability to fulfill your concept of the scene. You didn't
comment verbally, but I could see your comments. Had you embraced those comments instead of putting them in parentheses, they
would have merged into the character's life
and since this character is laced with problems and frustrations anyway, you would have
had it all going for you. That's what I
mean by walking the fence.

You were closer to BEING than Connie was, because I saw more of Danny and I want to make
a very important point about this. And that
is, as I told Connie, if somebody had walked
into this class tonight and seen the work,
they would have seen an enormous contrast between you and Connie. She was smooth, polished, certainly professional, whereas you
were erratic, filled with problems, somewhat
anti-social in your exclusion of the audience.
Bumpy. Your work was bumpy and hers was
smooth, and I'm sure the person watching
would have concluded that she was functioning
well as an actress and you were not. We've
learned to accept slick acting through conditioning. We see polished work on TV and films
and stage and that's what we learn to expect.
But when an actor is functioning organically
and honestly, he is anything but smooth. He
might even look somewhat "unprofessional"-
untechnical, undisciplined, untrained. This
system of BEING that we're struggling to reach
here is often ridiculed, because the approach
is unconventional. However, when you are
functioning totally from a BEING state, even
the severest critics of "Method" work are
awed, because the results are anything but

conventional. You're truly creating life on stage and people are not smooth in life. They are bumpy, unpredictable, easily derailed, and forget what they were going to say. That's the kind of reality that we as actors want to create on stage.

From Joan's Journal, 1972:

Combat with BEING Obstacles

Wednesday, July 5 . . . . . Performed part of my play in Eric's class tonight and afterwards my good friend, Emilie, who'd come to watch it, said I cry too much and it's wrong for the character of Bissie. I said Eric is directing and at this point he doesn't give a damn about the character. He wants me to find out who I am in relation to Bissie and express all of that. Emilie replied that she thinks my constant tears on stage come out of being too hard on myself and she thinks my self-punitive attitude is a cop-out, because it stops me from really experiencing the realities of what I'm feeling. She said I should take deliberate steps to be kinder to myself, be proud of what I'm doing and accept everything that I am because "everything is everything."

Many times Eric has told me the same thing, that I editorialize as I perform and my inner judgement stops me from BEING. Emilie's a dancer. Her disciplines are different from ours, but her remarks hit the same bull's eye as Eric's. I'm determined to change this pattern . . . . .

Saturday, July 29 . . . . . For three weeks Eric has been away doing a film. I've used the time off from rehearsals to practice a new habit of BEING. I want to get rid of my

32

negative self-analysis, that dubious crutch
I've leaned on all my life. So during these
three weeks, I've treated myself to all sorts
of pleasures. I bought a stereo. I had champagne and peach pie with some friends. I
made love. I enjoyed sweet moments with my
daughter at the beach. And every time that
stern voice inside me said, "You shouldn't
be wasting time. You should be working harder. Don't be silly. Don't be greedy. Why
are you doing that? Why did you say that?",
I deliberately silenced it and continued
living . . . . .

Tuesday, August 1 . . . . . I haven't worked
on my play today, but instead of berating
myself for that I lay down on the couch and
turned my stereo up high. In my head I could
hear Eric's voice saying, "Allow! Permit!
Accept! Include!" In time to the music. It
made me laugh out loud. I went to bed around
10:00 and awoke at 2:30 in the morning with a
sensation of unfinished business. Got up,
brushed my teeth, made tea and started working on the play . . . . .

Wednesday, August 2 . . . . . First rehearsal
with Eric since he's been away on the film.
He said he saw something he's never seen in
my work, a zest for it, a joy and lack of
commentary. Then I told him about these
three weeks of Non-Judgement Practice and he
confirmed that it's having results in my acting already. He said my behavior on stage
is more spontaneous and varied than before.
There's more creative excitement . . . . .

33

Different BEING States

JELLYBEAN:
HOW YOU WORK IN THE WORLD
IS HOW YOU WORK ON STAGE

When you've reached a BEING state, which means
BEING where you are at this moment in the here
and now, including everything that's going on
in you, then you are ready to act. What is
meant by the word "act" is to go from your
present state of BEING to the state of BEING
which the material demands. For instance,
your present state of BEING is: "I'm kind
of relaxed now, kind of depressed and heavy,
looking out of the window, tired and a little
down", but the emotional obligation of your
material might be a state of excitement and
joy, almost euphoria. The character in the
play has just been rewarded or has accomplished
something and feels very up about it. So you
have to find a way to go from this BEING state,
where you are now, to that BEING state. Sometimes the emotional demands of your material
are totally opposite to what you're feeling,
which gives you an enormous obligation. Many
actors fail because they try to jump from here
to there in one step. You might need to move
yourself through several interim steps in order
to go from your depression to joy.

Using available stimuli around you or working
for imaginary choices, you try to find ways to
make yourself less depressed and somewhat happier. You might look for things around the
room that make you feel better. You might
create a certain person in the room who would
make you feel very happy. Once you've achieved
an interim state of less depression and more
happiness, you are ready to influence this interim state through other choices and work toward a higher level of joy. Progressively you

34

encourage one BEING state to give way to another. Sometimes the BEING state you start with is so powerful and has such a grip on you that it's very difficult to affect it. At such times you will realize how important it is to know your instrument thoroughly, to have a large repertoire of choices and the skill to use them to get where you want to go. This ability will come only through hard work and daily practice.

When you are really BEING, one state carries over into the next and influences it like many colors running together and mixing, until your next BEING state becomes the dominant color. You've all seen actors who paint by the numbers, who are laughing one moment and the laughter abruptly stops and then you see anger. We call this impositional technique, a symptom of the anti-reality actor. In real life, the moment carries over and mixes with the next moment and you see the emotional subtleties of the change. This doesn't happen unless you're BEING. You must start in the totality of the BEING state, because you cannot create any life on stage or fulfill any scenic obligation until you first have a life going on. You cannot create life from the absence of life.

There's a natural process of responding to life. The process is stimulus-affect-response-expression. First you see, hear, taste, smell or feel something. That's the stimulus. It has some kind of an affect on you. Your instrument responds to that affect. You then express that response. The whole process happens in micro-seconds and it happens over and over again and this is referred to as living, which is BEING. If you are functioning from a BEING state, this natural process goes on without interference. BEING promotes stimulus-affect-response-expression, stimulus-affect-response-expression, stimulus-affect-response-expression.

The actor who premeditates his behavior, short-circuits the process anywhere along the line. He is so intent on executing his plan of how the scene should go that the stimulus may not even reach him. Or the stimulus may reach him but he's so committed to his intellectual concepts that he is unaffected by the stimulus. If he's busy simulating an affect, how can he be truly affected? Or he is affected by something that happens on the stage - his partner pats his cheek that night for the first time, but he doesn't allow himself to respond because he's imposing the behavior he feels should be there in the scene. He short-circuits the natural process of life, because he does not include his response to the pat on his cheek. If his responses are exclusive and unpremeditated, how can he respond with what he really feels? Instead of going with the organic response, his expression becomes prostituted by what he think the character should do or say. In this way, one denial sets up a chain reaction of denials until the lack of reality is epidemic.

When the actor short-circuits the natural process by assuming behaviors, by imposing attitudes, by "acting", he creates what is called "splits" in his instrument. There are all kinds of splits - vocal splits, emotional splits, physical and intellectual or any combination of these. The BEING state eliminates the possibility of splits or if the split occurs, BEING mends it.

Even if an actor achieves the BEING state and functions organically, there may be limitations in either the impressive or expressive areas which he needs to work on in order to make his

BEING states fuller and more colorful. For
instance, actors who are shy and quiet often
are extremely imaginative and affectable, but
unable to express anything. On the other
side of the coin there's the so-called extro-
vert, the exhibitionist who seems to flow
with expression but may not be at all aware
or sensitive. This kind of actor needs help
in the impressive area, exercises dealing
with his vulnerability.

Whatever the actor's problems are (and we all
have them at every stage of development),
BEING is ground zero. Implicit in BEING is
the inclusion of all your impulses, including
your problems as well as the infinite colors
of your emotional rainbow. The denial of
even one subtle shade of BEING diminishes
your total contribution as an artist. The
following exercises all directly relate to
BEING. Although these exercises have more
than one purpose, they are good ones to begin
with, because they are specifically designed
to help you to BE.

BEING Exercises

1. Personal Inventory

This is a stream-of-consciousness monologue,
which you do semi-audibly, so that you can
hear yourself talking, but no one else can.
You ask yourself, "How do I feel?", and then
you express your feelings and continue to
repeat the question. Do it for as little as
two minutes or as long as ten minutes and as
many times a day as you comfortably can. You
can do it at supermarkets, in your car, in a
restaurant waiting for a friend, really, anywhere. While the exercise is going on, things

will interfere with it, interrupt and take your attention away from the process. Include these things verbally in your monologue. For example "How do I feel? I just cleared my throat, getting ready to do this exercise. I feel obligated to do it. Taking a deep breathe. How do I feel? I'm looking for things to grab on to. My eyes are scanning the room. I feel anxious, a little tense in the chest. I hear a fly buzzing in the window. How do I feel? I feel excited about the job I got today. And I feel scared about it too, starting to work on it. How do I feel? I feel - uh - stuck. I don't know how I feel right now. I feel anxious about not knowing how I feel. That's how I feel! I feel anxious! Taking another deep breathe. I feel my stomach is bloated, I wish I could lose weight. I feel a little more in touch with how I feel, a little less anxious. I'm beginning to feel a little excitement rising up. . . wonder where that's coming from? How do I feel? I feel better, etc., etc." Personal Inventory, if practiced regularly, gets you in touch with what you're feeling and trains you to express everything that's going on moment-to-moment. Not every expression is verbal; it might be just vocal, like a sigh or a grunt. It alleviates tension and encourages a state of BEING.

2. One Person BEING

This is a good exercise to use following Personal Inventory. It's not necessary to continue the semi-audible process of asking yourself how you feel. Just BE! Allow and permit everything that you feel to express itself vocally, verbally and physically. Acknowledge and include all the obstacles that get in the way of simply going with what is. If, for example, you begin to comment on the propriety of your impulses and start to interfere with the expression of any group of feelings, then you should include your commentary, followed by whatever the true impulses are. The amazing thing about this process is that one expression gives way to the next and the next after that, and the flow of reality becomes compelling. Do the exercise sitting, standing, lying down, or whatever. Simply allow yourself to feel and express anything that's going on. *Try to find your personal gap between obligation and impulse.* Permit yourself to do what you feel and not what you think you should do. For additional ideas about how to do the exercise, refer to the taped dialogue in this chapter between E.J. and myself.

3. Personal Inventory II

The Personal Inventory exercise which we've already described is one of the better ways to become aware of what's going on inside you. You do it many times a day. Get in the habit of finding out how you feel at any given moment. Take inventory of how you're being affected by the objects around you, animate and inanimate. As we said before, you do the exercise audibly or semi-audibly by asking yourself, "How do I feel?" You may add the question, "How do I feel about that?"
After asking yourself, "How do I feel?", and answering the question, your next question should be, "Am I expressing how I feel and if not, why not?". This is an important question to add, because it prevents the exercise from becoming cerebral gymnastics. It turns it into a vigorous learning experience for you. If your answer is, "No, I'm not expressing how I feel.", then ask yourself, "What can I do to express it? How can I help myself express my feelings within the framework of the consequence? For example, "I feel like

39

punching him in the nose. Well, that's conse-
quential to someone else's well-being and to
mine also." When the consequences are too
large, you acknowledge your desire to punch
that person and you make a conscious choice
not to. The element of choice is not as
stifling as the element of suppression, stifling the impulse altogether and hiding it
from your awareness.

When you're asking yourself, "Am I expressing
how I feel and if not, why not?", the WHY is
the most important word. The WHY will open up
to you the knowledge of the things that stop
you from being yourself. "Because I'm afraid
of what they will think of me." If that answer keeps coming up, you've got to deal with
that as a problem. "Because I don't want them
to think I'm less than what I want them to
think I am." Once having found the answer to
your WHY, you then try to express as much as
you can. *You are entitled to all of your
emotions*. Nobody anywhere has the right to
deny what you feel. You're entitled to the
sum total of everything you are. And it's
not always nice. It's not always good or social or polite or concerned about others.
Sometimes you're loving and giving and you
love somebody who is not loving and giving
and you're disappointed. You're entitled to
that disappointment just as that person is
entitled not to love you.

*The minute you make rules about what you should
feel, those rules carry over to the stage or
camera.* They carry over because the rules are
the conditions by which you live. This doesn't
mean you should become an animal and hit people
over the head and steal from the Hollywood
Ranch Market. That's not what we mean at all.
There's a certain level of morality on which
people live. But all people have the license

40

to be themselves and we believe that actors have a special license, because feelings are our stock in trade.

4. I Am, I Want, I Need, I Feel

This is done aloud in a stream-of-consciousness fashion, but very rapidly, so that you don't have a chance to reflect or to premeditate on what you say. The purpose is to surprise yourself with what comes out. Start every sentence with one of the four statements, not necessarily in that order. For example: "I want to do this exercise. . . I am tense. . . I need to be good. . . I need to be seen. . . I feel self-conscious. . . I feel my fingers. . . I need money. . . I am what I am. . . I feel foolish. . . I want to laugh. . . I am laughing. . . I need love. . . I want to know what I want. . . I feel full . . . I need space. . . I am running out of things . . . I am looking at the floor. . . !" The exercise is purposely designed to channel your impulses into the format of "I Am, I Want, I Need, I Feel." When you respond to the specific line of self-questioning, your awareness of the moment to moment realities becomes clearer. The important element is the impulsiveness of your response. If you take a beat to think about the response, you might just be filling the blank with your conditioned thought rather than your real feeling. It is important to remember that if you go blank, say the first thing that comes to your mind no matter how illogical or nonsensical it may seem. You may repeat "I Am _____, I Want _____, I Need _____, I Feel _____," many times, but encourage yourself to go back and forth between the four statements.

41

5. What Do I Want?

The purpose of this exercise is to find out
what you want here and now, but also in the
larger sense. The exercise differs from I Am,
I Want, I Need, I Feel because it is not done
impulsively. The reason here is to find out
what the underlying life is (i.e., "What do I
want in a more complete sense?"). The emphasis is on a more intellectual and philosophi-
cal overview of what you want in life. It is
necessary to start on a here and now level to
encourage a free flow and avoid the tendency
to become heady. The exercise is done like
Personal Inventory, but with the question,
"What do I want?", instead of "How do I Feel?"
For example: "What do I want? I want to find
out what I want. What do I want? I want to
be happier than I am now. I want to work more.
I want to be good. I want people to respect
me. What do I want? I want not to care about
those things. I want to be successful." If
you wish, you can include this exercise in the
Personal Inventory instead of doing it separately.

The intention of "The Method" is the achieve-
ment of organic reality on the stage. All
reality on the stage is ostensibly created
from the inner life of the actor, from his
own living experiences. The method and its
inherent techniques are structured to this
end, however, the system does not tell the
actor how this is achieved. Since all people
are different and have problems that are unique to themselves, how can any formulized
system work the same for everyone? The answer is that it cannot, which is why "The
Method" is not widely used or respected. The
search and process of finding yourself and
achieving a BEING state - that is to say,
A STATE OF BEING OURSELVES, TOTALLY, is what

this book offers to the actor. BEING is the
primary and basic foundation to a creative
process. Once the actor arrives at his bedrock reality, the truth, his truth here and
now, in this moment and at this place, he is
ready to affect that truth and change it to
anything the material requires. BEING is
not a state you achieve immediately, it is
a way of life that evolves out of much work
and experimentation. Besides requisite ingredients of talent and commitment as an
artist, you must have COURAGE. You must be
willing to take chances and sometimes suffer
the consequences of your actions, to pursue
your individuality and to make your statement in life and on the stage. Remember, no
one ever contributed lasting things to the
world without taking chances and often in-
curring resentment and controversy from the
people around them. Living and acting are
all too often separated and they mustn't be.
The exercises in this book are specifically
constructed to become your tools to bridge
the gap between you and your work. The awe-
some impact of completely BEING on the stage
is thrilling to an audience. When you achieve
BEING, every part of you knows it! The feeling is unmistakable.

If you use the work prescribed here, practice
these exercises daily and make the approach
part of your life, you will experience this
magical state of BEING. The results of this
work are filled with rewards and wonderful
surprises.

II

GETTING READY TO GET READY

Tension: How It Affects the Actor
_____

According to the dictionary, tension is the
act of stretching or straining, being strain-
ed to stiffness, a state of tightness, mental
strain, nervous anxiety. Without getting into the physiological origins of tension -
that's for a medical book - we'll concern
ourselves with it as it relates to acting.
Tension is a state of BEING that all actors
experience and it's usually something that
the actor will have to deal with all his life.
It manifests itself in thousands of ways, in
as many different ways as there are actors.
It can be a tightening of the muscles in
various parts of the body - back of the neck,
shoulders, hands, arms and so forth, - sweaty
palms, dry mouth, "butterflies", trembling
hands, difficulty in breathing, pressure in
the chest, and on and on. The actor feels
enormously uncomfortable, awkward and self-
conscious. These are some of the symptoms
of physical tension.

Mental tension affects the actor's thinking.
He suffers from either a conglomeration of
thoughts and can't remember his lines, or
from the absence of thought, the inability
to think anything. He is spaced out, stoned,
the eyes are vacant, panicked, and there's a
tightening around the eyelids. Physical and
mental tension usually occur together, both
states crippling the actor, making him helpless

on stage, incapable of being affected or responding, unable to function on an organic level.

What then can we do with this enemy? Why does it happen? What causes it? And is it completely bad? Or does it have some good aspects? Can it be used? If so, how? These questions and many others will be discussed throughout the book.

Tension is the actor's Number One problem, because unless he knows how to alleviate it, he can't proceed to anything else. Many actors never get to the nucleus of their real talent because they function above their tension. Tension might be compared to a corked bottle. Let us imagine for a moment that a human being is like a bottle filled with many emotions and impulses. If you were to put a stopper on that bottle, nothing could come out. Tension acts as a stopper and everything below that stopper is trapped and bottled up. The actor then must impose a behavior above that stopper and this kind of behavior leads only to intellectual and conceptual acting. You cannot play an idea!

Actors become quite facile at functioning above the cork, never confronting the real life underneath. They develop trademark behavior, elements of "personality", mannerisms that they become well-known for and even hired for. However, in denying their tension and what lies beneath it, they are robbing themselves of ninety per cent of their talent. Their behavior on stage is conceptual, impositional, representational and predictable.

You've all heard actors admit that just before going on stage they experience a lot of tension, but it disappears like magic as soon as

they set foot on the boards. If you're one
of these actors, we must assume that you become involved at that split second and have
gotten rid of your pre-entrance tension. If
that's the case, fine. You're in good shape
and if it happens that way for you all the
time, just skip this chapter entirely.

However, you may be deluding yourself into
believing you're involved. You may have
suppressed your tension. You may not even
be aware of its presence. This kind of delusion and false sense of well-being is dangerous to you as an actor, keeping you from
reaching into the well of your real contribution.

Half the battle in conquering a human problem
is first to recognize that it exists. Too
many actors deny the existence of tension in
themselves. They suppress it so completely
that they can only function on a superficial
level, a facilitated behavior that can sometimes be quite interesting, but can never be
real and organic. You've seen actors who are
apparently relaxed. They seem calm and in
complete control, but their behavior somehow
isn't quite real or believable. They're re-
acting too broadly perhaps, doing more than
they should be doing. Their eyes may be
glassed over and they stare at your chin as
they speak. This kind of actor, seemingly
calm and relaxed, exudes self-confidence all
over the stage. You watch him saunter jaun-
tily downstage and pick up a glass or a
cigarette and then suddenly you observe that
he can't stop his hand from trembling. His
knees may also be doing quite a little number
of their own. Many actors become adept at
suppressing their tension. Through years of
experience they've learned to impose a studied
naturalness on top of this suppression. These

actors are often referred to as competent performers, troupers, pros that go out there and there and say their jokes and grab their money and run. Competent they may be by some standards, but exciting they will never be!

On the otherhand, there's the actor who is all too aware of his tension. He knows he's miserable, but because he doesn't understand his tension or know how to help himself, it cripples him, renders him incapable of working. He literally falls apart. In a field as competitive as the theatre it is detrimental to "show" tension. It may well cost you a job. If you don't show confidence in yourself, they won't have confidence in you and they'll get somebody else instead. Therefore, we become conditioned to hiding it and after years of doing just that, we succeed in hiding it even from ourselves.

It is just as easy to deal with your tension as it is to impose relaxation. It's simply a matter of redirecting your efforts. You may be thinking at this point, "That's easier said than done." Quite true! It's much easier to talk about dealing with it than actually doing so, but tension is a demon that will be with you your entire life. Don't despair. Don't feel hopeless. Tension is also an indication of your talent. It is the manifestation of unexpressed emotions, bottled up impulses, all your personal responses to the world. The mor tension you have, the more there is going on inside of you that is not coming out. Tension is the result of an interruption in the natural process of Stimulus-Affect-Response-Expression. Your tension is evidence that you are strongly affected by a wide range of stimuli. That's what is meant by the quote, "Tension is talent." Usually people with extreme tension problems are people who are extremely sensitive and affectable.

48

Learning a craft which you can depend on, encouraging a faith in your talent and knowing your own tension problems and how to deal with them, are all important factors in your development. Suppose you go to a doctor for some corrective surgery. He will diagnose the problem, find the right tools to work with and correct the trouble. He will have very little tension about doing his job, because he is sure of his skill and his knowledge of what to do and how to do it. Like the doctor, an actor must also have a craft he can count on. Then, and only then, can he approach his job with the same confidence as the surgeon.

From Joan's Journal, Tuesday, April 4, 1972:

Identifying and Dealing with Tension

First rehearsal with Eric on my play. As I opened my front door for him and said, "Hi", I felt that old knot of fear in my stomach that I used to have for every Broadway audition. It lies near where I breath and spreads like a fishnet to all parts of my body so that I'm trapped in total self-consciousness.

Eric was his usual self, but I kept reading rejection behind his calm demeanor. That's how I trap myself into that net. I attribute to the director a stream of negative thoughts about me. . . "She's not a good actress, but she looks the part. . . God, what a drag. She doesn't know anything. . . Well, she's neurotic and lonely and getting old. I'll just be patient with her. . ."

There was a time when these negative fantasies polluted almost every piece of work I did. That's how I got fired from my first Broadway musical. From the first day of

49

rehearsal I was convinced the director hated
me and the conviction spread through my limbs
like blood poisoning. I tripped over the
scenery, sprained my ankle, got laryngitis
and conjunctivitis until finally, in Phila-
delphia, he fired me, which my self-hating
mind had willed him to do from the beginning.

I didn't know at the time that tension was my
blood poisoning, the cause of all my maladies.
Now, after two years of study with Eric, these
cruel fantasies no longer have the upper hand.
I know how to help myself. I can get involved
in the work now, feel positive and excited
about it, even though the dark thoughts still
gleam below like dirty water at the bottom of
the well.

Causes of Tension

This excerpt is an example of some of the major
causes of tension in actors.

1. Joan's anxiety about the "First Rehearsal"
    (I found in working with her on the play
    that she had anxiety before each rehearsal.
    As we worked, it became less.)

2. Her desire to succeed and be good in the
    play.

3. Her lack of specific craft at the time and
    her lack of faith in the craft that she had.

4. Her fear of my judgement and mind-reading
    negative thoughts into me.

5. Her basic insecurity about being enough.

6. Physical manifestations of tension which,
    themselves, caused more tension.

The causes of tension are infinite. Some of the more common causes are the actor's ego-state, his insecurities, his need to succeed and be good, the fear of failure and the consequences of failing, the absence of craft and the lack of faith in the instrument. The actor's ego-state is very important to his ability to function on stage. If the ego-state is low, he'll have minimal faith in himself and, therefore, maximum anxiety and fear of failure, which leads to tension. When you are at peace with yourself and you feel you're a worthy person with much to offer, then it's much easier to be successful at anything you do and you'll experience much less tension. In fact, it might simply be the pleasant sensation of excitement.

Some actors are in a perpetually low ego-state due to childhood conditioning and other reasons. Other actors who tend to be more confident may at certain times be overcome by life - losing a job, going through a divorce, waking up one morning feeling hopeless about the future. At these moments, if you have to get on stage and act, you'll have a great deal of tension. You can either deal specifically with the tension or with the causes of it - your low ego-state, or with both problems. You'll find in this book a large number of exercises for building a better ego-state quickly. Of course, you seldom can define the exact reasons for a high or a low ego-state and it's really not important to try. What's important is to get your ego to where you want it to be for the work you have to do. Many kinds of ego preparations will be described and you will discover many of your own. As the saying goes, "If it works, use it!"

Talent is an oblique thing made up of many

fears, frustrations and unfulfilled desires. Insecurity, another major cause of tension, is bred by these particular elements of talent. Talent is a beautiful gift and has many other wonderful elements but, unfortunately, it can stand in its own way. Everybody on earth has insecurities of one kind or another. And one insecurity can often spread like a disease through your whole spirit. An actor's insecurities can cripple him, stop him from being able to do anything. Craft is the antidote. Having a craft will enable you to live with your insecurities and function, not in spite of them, but in terms of them. Insecurity is the feeling that you don't know how to do, or that you cannot do what is expected of you. BUT if you know what do do - and you know that you know - and you know HOW to do it, then you will do it and not be insecure about it.

The need to succeed and be good looms large as another cause of tension in actors. Once upon a time in Japan, a young man desirous of learning the art of the Samurai, consulted with the oldest and greatest master of Samurai. He sai "Honorable Master, I wish to become the greatest Samurai in the world. I will study diligently. How long will it take me?" The Maste replied, "Ten years." The student was shocked "No, no, Honorable Master, you don't understand I will live, eat, sleep and breath the Samurai I will think of nothing else! You see, I must be great. If I live, eat, sleep and breath the Samurai and think of nothing else, then how long will it take me?" The Master's answer was, "In that case, twenty years."

JELLYBEAN: SOMETIMES LESS IS MORE

Impatience and the need to succeed and be good are demons. It is quite natural that people want to succeed in what they do. Much of our

personal and financial gain comes from a job
well done. Even from childhood a certain
competitiveness is instilled in us by our
parents. People often come to the profession of acting out of a need for love and
recognition and admiration. Their upper-
most need is to be good. If an actor is
mature enough to train his instrument and if
he has talent and is willing to work for many
years, trying and failing and succeeding and
failing and trying some more, then he will
be "good" creatively and he will achieve sat-
isfaction in his art.

If, however, your need to be good is so strong
that it prevents you from experimentation and
squelches your courage to try things which
might lead to failure, then you will cling to
the things which you know you can do. By
playing it safe your real talent will atrophy
and your unique contribution will never be
born. The great people of history in any
field have been those with the courage to
take chances, those who have investigated
and questioned things, those who have made
decisions in the face of any kind of opposi-
tion. You, the actor, are unique and individual, different from any other actor in
the world. Your greatest contribution to
the theatre will be what you can give of
yourself to it. If you are willing to fail,
and by failing, to learn, then you may discover the full dimensions of your talent.
However, it is difficult to find this willingness in ourselves, because we are not
allowed many failures as actors, before pro-
ducers become reluctant to hire us.

The actor must have a place to fail. There
are workshops, classes, experimental the-
atres all over. These are the places where
we can allow ourselves the NECESSITY of

failing. The peculiar paradox is that when we
are ready to accept failure as a necessary
part of growth, we succeed more often than
those who will not allow themselves to be bad.
Tension is nurtured by the need to succeed and
be good. If the need is so strong that the
very thought of failure is unbearable, then
quite a tension problem will result.

Among the most prevalent causes of tension are
the absence of craft and the lack of faith in
the instrument. Craft and faith are interre-
lated. Faith in your instrument comes from
the security of having a concrete craft. It's
quite possible to have a lot of faith without
craft and, conversely, a lot of craft without
faith. Either way you're in trouble. It's
true that faith alone may carry you a great
distance, but faith based on accidental, hit-
or-miss skill is not dependable. If you have
craft, but no faith in it, then you can't use
what you know.

The beginning actor is an interesting phenomenon. He has little or no training and often
a great deal less tension than the experienced
actor who has worked many years in the theatre
The beginner will often "jump in" courageously
and commit himself totally. He hasn't discovered the complexities of creation. He knows
very little of what is at stake and has a
blind faith in his great intuitive talent. He
or she is not "on the spot", because there
isn't any spot yet! This explains why many
actors feel they were better off before they
began to study and, peculiarly, they may have
been freer. But as their realization of what
is expected grows, their freedom turns to ter-
ror unless they've been building a craft.

The ideal state is to believe that the craft
you're learning and using is a workable approa

to acting and that it will do for you, personally, what you want it to do. Your craft
and your faith in it will come from trial-
-failure-success, work, work, work, work!

Another phenomenon related to tension is the
actor who can't function *without it*. This
is a very common and dangerous tension problem. This kind of actor works directly off
his tension and cannot act unless he feels a
great turmoil within. He's in fine shape on
opening night when there is always a great
deal of tension. He feels good on the first
and second days of shooting a film because,
in the midst of all the uncertainties, he's
thrown on the spot in front of the camera
and has to come through with a performance.
But as he becomes more secure, his tension
naturally becomes less and he has to stimulate it artificially in order to act. I call
this acting problem "Theatrical Hysteria" or
"Ass Energy". The actor's creative energy is
really just nervous tension.

He doesn't recognize it as such and that's
what makes Theatrical Hysteria so dangerous.
Some actors have based entire careers on Ass
Energy. You've seen them. The contorted
faces, the clenched teeth, muscles stretched
to the breaking point, the constant cryers
and sobbers. The actor himself is convinced
that what he's feeling is great emotional
experiences coming from deep within him.
Without this sensation he feels naked. When
his natural tension dissipates and he must
artificially manufacture it, he thinks he's
"preparing". What he is actually doing is
giving himself a diarrhetic flow of tension,
which passes for and takes the place of what
he really feels. The tragedy is that he robs
himself of genuine emotional experience.

55

The "Actress"

Recently in a private lesson I was working with a professional actress who is frequently seen on television. She was preparing a monologue from "Virginia Woolf". She started by pulling herself together, sitting upright in the chair, taking deep breaths, readying herself for what she knew was to come. She stared at an empty chair as if creating an imaginary person. Within seconds her eyes filled with tears. Her chest began to heave. The muscle at the side of her jaw pulsed in and out like a metronome. She exploded into a flow of words heavy with emotion. For five minutes she went on, standing up and beating the air with her fists. When she had finished she sat down and again pulled herself together Melodramatically, as if the experience had just been too much for her, she turned to me and I saw on her face a radiant self-satisfaction. She said, "Well? What do you think?"

I took several moments before I decided to tell her what I thought. It was obvious to me she'd been working this way for a long time and liking it. For my criticism to get through to her I'd really have to be honest with her. I decided that her process of work was infinitely more destructive to her than anything I could tell her.

She said, smiling, "Eric, I'm waiting."

I said, "I didn't believe one micro-second of what I saw. It was nonsense."

Her face fell. She was shocked. "What do you mean? How can you say that? I _felt_ all those things!"

"I don't question that you felt something.

56

But do you know why you and I are in conflict about the work? Why I think you're
looking for ways to cut and run from here?
Because I don't give you what you want. I
don't tell you how talented and beautiful
you are and how excited I am by your emotional outbursts when you do "Virginia Woolf"
and "Dylan" and "Moony's Kid Don't Cry". I
don't tell you that because it's all general
neurotic emotion. Its origin is general.
When you get on the stage to act, you magically and mystically fill up with all this
conglomerated emotion, the tears, the rage,
the retching. And you think this is the
flow, the mainline flow of your talent. But
it's actually your tension, your fear of
failure, your anxiety and your need for love
and acceptance and your desire to be acclaimed
as a creative artist, rolled up into a ball
of theatrically hysterical emotion. You pay
lip service to working for a choice, but
actually you take that conglomerated, neurotic emotion and box it into "Virginia Woolf"
or wrap it into "Dylan". It's fraudulent,
impure. You've been 'passing' for a finely
tuned emotional instrument, but in reality
you're a fraud. You're short-changing yourself ninety-eight cents out of every talent
dollar you possess. No, I'm not going to
give you what you want. I want to give you
what you need. And you need to let go of
what you depend on and run the risk of getting nothing, until that nothing becomes
reality."

Dealing With Tension

We have now discussed some of the major causes
of tension, though certainly not all of them.
You'll find the rest of this chapter rich in
remedies. At the risk of being redundant, we

stress the importance of recognizing your tension, acknowledging it and then proceeding systematically to alleviate it. As soon as you ask a question, you will begin getting answers. Where am I tense? Where in my body do I feel discomfort? Where is it moving to now? It's logical that the more questions you ask the more answers you get.

Each person has different tension points. Usually the tension will find its way to the same points and once you become aware of these places you'll find it easier to help yourself. Pinpoint the areas, admit them and encourage the tension to express itself. "I feel tight in my shoulders. Hello, tension in the shoulders. I know you're there. My knees are shaking. Okay, knees. Shake." If you find your hands are trembling, encourage them to do that. Let it show. When you feel all your shaking and trembling and tightness has reached a peak, then simply ask those parts of your body to relax. Let your hands hang loosely and be pulled naturally by gravity.

Your tension points are the areas that the tension finds in hopes of getting out. It must be released somehow. If there is a denial of its presence and it is stifled at every outlet it will bounce around inside and totally cut the actor off from either being affected by a stimulus or having an honest response to one. The actor who shows his tension is better off than the one who has it under control, because when it's closer to the surface it can be spotted and dealt with. Identify the tension in all parts of your body in the same way - face, chest, stomach, pelvis, legs, feet, etc.

There are thousands of ways to deal with tension problems. Try anything that you feel might do the job. At times one thing will

work and at other times the very thing that
worked before will fail. It's wise to know
and to have tried many techniques. Knowing
what to use depends largely on knowing yourself, knowing what kinds of things affect
you, and when.

Besides identifying and acknowledging your
tension, you will find you can also help
yourself by getting involved. Tension is
usually the result of being concerned with
yourself. It follows that if you can trans-
fer that concern away from yourself, you'll
get rid of your self-consciousness. Ask
yourself simple questions such as: "How
many different colors can I count on this
stage?" Count them. "How many set pieces
do I see here?" Count them. Relate to the
objects around you by asking personal questions about them such as, "What does that
couch mean to me? Have I ever seen one like
it? In whose house?" Often the answers to
your questions will kick off a certain behavioral relationship to these objects. Ask a
question about the people you're working
with. "What are the most attractive features about that girl? Who does she remind
me of? Is there any resemblance between her
and any other woman I know? If so, what
features are alike and what features are
different?" And on and on. If you allow
the responses that have been stimulated by
these questions to express themselves, you
will begin to function quite organically and
creatively.

Sometimes the tension will be stuffed down
inside you, compacted into many layers. It
may be impossible to connect with it in any
of the ways we've mentioned. It will be necessary to do a more active and drastic preparation. Here you'll find useful the

Abandonment group of exercises.

When your ego is involved and affecting your
state of tension, then choose any of the exercises in the Ego group. In the meantime, you
might take yourself off the spot by asking
yourself questions such as: "Is it possible
for me to please everybody? Of course not.
So why try? Can I do anything about the way
people think? Not really. Who must I ultimately please?" You know the answer to that
one and you'll discover that you are the one
who expects the most from you. Why not just
begin with the goal of pleasing yourself, and
if you get close to doing that, you will please
many people along with yourself.

As you become more involved in a specific craft
a creative approach to your work will emerge
and some of your reasons for acting may undergo
a change. You might find that your relationship to acting is now on a deeper level than
what originally attracted you to the art. You
might find that in the excitement of creation
lies the real fulfillment of your needs. Your
acting will then acquire a more courageous at-
tack. You will be achieving tasks that you've
set for yourself rather than working for praise
acceptance and recognition. As the obligation
to succeed diminishes, so will the tension
caused by it.

The actor should have a group of exercises that
work for him or her, depending on the situation
and personal need. In my classes I like to
start with physical relaxation exercises such
as Logey, Rag Doll, Tense and Relax. But other
exercises, which we'll talk about here, relieve
physical tension as a result of getting involved in something other than yourself, or as
a result of large expurgative actions. The
actor learns what's most effective for him and

collects his own tools.

                    JELLYBEAN:
    IN ORDER TO ACT YOU MUST BE RELAXED.
  IN ORDER TO RELAX YOU MUST HELP YOURSELF
  TO RELAX.   IN ORDER TO BE, YOU MUST INCLUDE
    EVERYTHING YOU ARE.   IT TAKES COURAGE.

The Physical Relaxers

The exercises in this catagory deal primarily
with the existence of physical tension, although many of the exercises in every catagory may serve more than one purpose.

1.   Tense and Relax

Lie down on the floor, or remain standing if
necessary. Starting from your feet, tighten
slowly by degrees each part of your body,
holding it tight until your whole body is rigid. Then from the top of your head start
relaxing by degrees slowly, until you return
to where you started. Do this two or three
times. The exercise forces your muscles to
relax by tiring them and it also teaches your
body to recognize the varying degrees of tension so that when you experience tension on
stage, you'll be more specifically aware of
it and able to deal with it. It's essential
to learn how to do this for yourself, because
it takes a lot of muscular tension to keep
impulses suppressed, and when this muscular
tension is relieved, the impulses flow.

2. Logey

Logey is one of my invented words and to me
it means heavy, slothfull and lethargic. This
is the physical state and feeling you want to
achieve. Lie down on the floor, flat on your

back at first. Later you'll find your own Logey
positions. Become aware of the weight of your
body, the weight of your head, of your limbs, of
your thorax, your pelvis, thighs, legs. People
support their weight through muscular tension
and energy so that we never think that the head
weighs fifteen pounds or more, but if we release
that support, that head feels heavy. Start the
exercise, becoming aware of your normal weight.
Then increase and expand the sense of your weigh
until you feel even heavier. Test your Logey by
lifting your arms one at a time and letting them
fall of their own weight. Do this with all
parts of the body, feeling the pull of gravity
on each part. By removing the body's support,
you remove its physical tension.

3. Rag Doll

Stand up on both feet and from the top of your
head, let yourself be pulled toward the ground,
one vertebra at a time, until you finally crum-
ple on the floor in a rag heap. Do it slowly,
letting your arms hang loosely at your sides.
When you reach the knees, bend them.

4. Original Being

This exercise requires more time - about an
hour - and it does more than just relax you.
It sensitizes you and makes you keenly aware
of things around you that you've never noticed.
Do it either sitting up or lying down, preferably lying down. Clear your mind of thoughts
and try to achieve a kind of wakeful sleep.
Than slowly awaken, as if for the first time.
You are fully grown with your normal intelligence and musculature, but no prior experience
of anything at all. You see, hear, feel, taste,
smell everything as if for the first time. You
have your own muscular abilities, but without
the knowledge of how even to move your hand.

Richard Hatch doing an "original being" exercise.

All of this must be discovered and learned.
Original Being can be used for other purposes
besides relaxation. It's an anti-intellec-
tual, anti-premeditative process. After you
do it, you realize how many things you take
for granted and how often you premeditate
your responses to things and to people.

5. Deep Breathing

Lie down and breathe more deeply with each
breath you take. Exhale as fully as you in-
hale. Breathe as if your body was a hollow
vessel and all the air you breathe will finally reach down to the soles of your feet.

6. Abandonment

This exercise is useful when you're enormously tense and you have to blast through your
barricades. It is large, physically and vocally. Clear a good space for yourself in
the room. Remove necklaces, glasses, watches,
and any object that could hurt you. Do it on
a carpet or a fairly soft ground surface.
With abandonment, hurl yourself into what
might resemble having a physical "fit", kick-
ing, flailing your body in every direction,
screaming, howling and being as vocally aban-
doned as you are physically. The exercise
should go on until you're spent. When it's
over, you might cry or laugh or experience a
large emotional expurgation of some kind.
This exercise, besides getting rid of your
tension, can also be used to get down deeper
and free reluctant emotions.

7. Dump

This is based on Dr. George Bach's Vesuvius
exercise, and like the Abandonment, it's also
a large expurgative. Start expressing all

your frustrations, dissatisfactions, angers, disappointments, needs, desires, until you achieve an eruptive flow of all that has been suppressed. You are then free to move past it and go on to other things.

8.   Dealing With The Demon

I found out something about tension in working with actors in the classroom and in commercial situations. Once you identify tension, verbally acknowledge its presence in you and what it's doing to you at that moment, the tension moves around. It's elusive. You might feel it in your chest, identify it and then it jumps down to your legs. It finds another hiding place. I invented this exercise to train actors to hunt the demon - and it is a demon - tension is the original demon - and to expose it. For instance, the actor might be feeling a kind of general relaxation, but when he starts to speak, his voice quivers. The tension has gone into his voice-box. I acted in a film recently and before the take, I'd done preparations, felt relaxed, and related to the actress working with me, ready to do the scene. Then they called "Action" and two lines later, the demon put his hand on the back of my neck and my whole head started to shake.

The enemy to tension is exposure. If you allow it to stay hidden, it compounds itself. But if you expose it publicly, out loud, you no longer have the need to be better off than you really are. *Everybody knows you're tense and instead of the charade, you can get down to the business of ridding yourself of it.*

This exercise is also done in a stream-of-consciousness fashion, as many of the exercises are, in order to stimulate a moment-to-moment flow of reality. Verbally - out loud or semi-

Karen Gehrman doing abandoment exercise to get loose and ready to work.

67

audibly - and preferably in front of the people you're working with, chase your demon as it scurries through your body. For example: "Oh, I feel tension in the back of my neck. Hello there, Demon. Oh, it just moved down to my shoulder. It's in my right shoulder. That's funny, I just became aware that my stomach is a little jumpy. It's down there now. It's both in my shoulders and my stomach now. I'm looking around, seeing everybody working on the set. Who's that person the director's talking to? Oh, oh, I just felt it insidiously creeping into my back. Hello, Demon. I know where you are. My throat is closing up a little bit. I'm taking a deep breath and it's okay. I know you're there. I know all the places where you are and I'm going to allow you to be there, because I can't deny you. . ." and so forth, until you feel ready to work.

Joan uses the following variation of Dealing With The Demon, which is based on a Gestalt exercise. "I locate the Demon outside of myself. I place it on a chair or on some object across from me and then I talk to it as Joan. I say things like, 'I'm sick and tired of you, Black Fear. You've plagued me all my life. You turn my bowels to water and make my throat dry and take all the fun out of acting. I exhaust myself trying to get rid of you, but you always come back.' And then I switch roles and become the Demon talking to Joan. I'll say something like, 'Oh, come off it, Joan, you're kidding yourself trying to be an actress. You're middle-aged and you haven't made it and you'll never make it. You missed your calling. You really should have been somebody's fat wife in the suburbs.' And then I'll be Joan again and talk back to it. 'Stop that! You get away from me! I'm doing what I love to do and you're not going to drag me down!'' I'll spend sometimes as long as a half hour on this dialogue and by the end of it I feel freer, more centered in my self-esteem, less victimized by a vague enemy and the reason is because I've made that enemy very specific. The dialogue exposes to me the kind of negative self-talk that I inflict upon my faith. It objectifies my Demon.

JELLYBEAN: IF I AM NOT FOR ME,
THEN WHO WILL BE?

9. Expose Innermost Feelings in Jibberish

Sometimes we get tense not because we're on th spot, but because we have a mountain of unexpressed feelings and impulses that we have not vented. A lot of these things might be so pri vate or personal that to vent them in words might have undesireable consequences. You nee to express these pent-up feelings so that you can get beneath and beyond them to other kinds of life. You can express them in jibberish, releasing your impulses without violating your privacy. This exercise is most effective, as many of these exercises are, when done in fron of other people.

10. The Ingestion Exercise

I devised this exercise in a private lesson with an actor and then later found it valuable for many actors. It is non-verbal, but very vocal. With gesture and sound, you take into your body and ingest all the objects around you, growing larger and louder and stronger and more powerful with each ingestion, until you feel you're a giant ball of energy and power. This exercise is exciting to watch when done well because in a minute you see a human being grow in stature and become enormously compelling on stage.

Joan Hotchkiss "dealing with the demon" during a rehearsal of Legacy.

71

The Involvement Group

The exercises so far have related to dealing
with the self, which requires self-involvement. But often tension can be relieved by
getting involved in something outside of
yourself. The following exercises fall into
this category.

11. Taking Responsibility for Others

Taking Responsibility for Others is designed
to get you off the spot by involving you with
things outside of yourself. Do it standing
up, using the people around you, your rehearsal group or classroom. Express what you observe about these people as selflessly as
possible, excluding the word "I" as much as
you can and also excluding any personal re-
lations you might have with them. Try objectively to help each person be better off than
he is right now, giving specifically constructive suggestions. The word "responsibility"
is the key to this exercise. If you really
feel responsible for helping the other person,
then something immediately becomes more important to you than you and your tension.

12. Total Selflessness

This is similar to the one above except that
you don't take responsibility for helping anyone. You relate to your environment, observing it and commenting on it without ever using
the pronoun "I" or relating anything back to
yourself. For example, "That's a beautiful
bush. It smells marvelous. You really seem
to be creatively involved in what you're doing
This place has a fantastic view, doesn't it?
You don't seem to take advantage of the beauty
around you. . ." And so forth. Just because

you're excluding the word "I" does not mean
that you are not affected by the things you're
observing. The exercise usually succeeds in
getting you out of yourself.

13. The Trivial Trio

Say the Alphabet Backwards

Count Your Own Heartbeats

Say a Line of Dialogue Backwards

These exercises are simple devices for placing
your energy in an area away from your concerns
with self.

14. Threshold of Interest

This exercise is non-verbal. Look around you
and investigate the things that interest you
with all five senses, going from object to object only as you are impelled to. This encourages you to get involved in things outside of
yourself without obligations.

Internal Awareness

An actor's preparation must include a working
process to increase his awareness, his awareness of what's going on inside him and what's
happening in the world around him. The more
things you're aware of, the more things you're
affected by. The more things you're affected
by, the more kinds of emotional life you experience, and, therefore, the more levels of
life you have to draw from in creating the
behavior of different kinds of people.

At any given moment, billions of things are

happening both inside and out. Naturally
you can't be aware of even a fraction of all
that - the sound all the way down to the
sounds of silence, the smells, the colors
and shapes around you and the infinite spec-
trum of your inner feelings about all these
things, your personal point of view. But
if you keep stretching your awareness, you'll
have a larger and larger living canvas. Sti-
mulus-affect, response, and expression - this
is the natural order. The greater the number
of things that you're aware of and available
to, the richer your talent.

All of the following exercises in the Internal
Awareness Group are explained in detail in
Chapter I. As has been said before, many of
these exercises are multi-purposed.

15. Personal Inventory I

16. Personal Inventory II

17. What Do I Want?

18. I Am, I Want, I Need, I Feel

External Awareness

Since a large part of eliminating tension is
based on involvement away from the problem,
becoming aware and related to things around
you is a natural progression. This group of
exercises relates to objects, places, and
people outside of yourself.

19. Nature Walk

This is a rich investigation of your environment. Take a walk outdoors, ideally in a place
where nature is overwhelming - the mountains,
the sea, the snows. But your own backyard is
fine too. Become aware of everything around
you on every sensory level - smell, taste,
touch, sight, sound. Pick up a leaf and study
the vein structure. Smell it. Crush it in
your fingers and feel the texture. Taste it.
Lose yourself in the life of that leaf. Then
broaden your awareness to include the fullness
of the whole tree, the distance between the
tree and the mountain, the shadows from the
sunlight, the sun on your face, the way the
ground feels under your feet as you walk. Explore everything you can and allow yourself to
be affected emotionally. You may be affected
in many different ways. You might·be overwhelmed by the smallness of your size in relation to the universe or elated by the fra-
grances.

20. Awareness Levels

This is a running verbal account of all the
levels of your sensory awareness as they happen. It encourages your gradual and increasing awareness of the subtleties and complexities of the immediate environment. Don't
evaluate, analyse or comment on how you feel
about any of it. "That dog barking is terri-
bly loud. A plane overhead, faint. Now I
hear the motorcycle. Bird just flew out from
under the eaves. Bird twittering. Door
slammed in the house. Odor of the flowered
bush and now it went away. Cool breeze across
my left knee. Plane very faint overhead.
Breeze moving the bushes. Noticed the pattern
of the bricks in the patio. Some kind of
fumble coming from somewhere. Fingerpads sore

from typing." As you do this exercise, you'll become more aware of increasing subtleties in your awareness, levels beneath the levels.

21. Observe, Wonder and Perceive

Like Personal Inventory, this is a craft-back-bone exercise and has many purposes. For now we'll confine ourselves to what it can do for your awareness. You can do it silently, semi-audibly or audibly with people. Start simply by observing the things you observe and express that. "I observe that you look tired." Then you might add, "I wonder, are you tired? Are you not feeling well? I perceive from your behavior that you don't want to answer that question. You look angry. I wonder if you're angry. I wonder, do you color your hair? You look like you've been working hard. The exercise is a monologue. It doesn't have to relate to people and it isn't necessary to preface each wonderment or perception with I Wonder or I Perceive. But use these phrases at first to keep from slipping back into self-involvement.

22. Farmers' Market

I call this the Farmers' Market Exercise because I used to take my class there every Wednesday morning to learn to observe human behavior. The Farmers' Market is loaded with people of all nationalities and from all parts of our country. It's a bountiful place in which to do this exercise, but you can do the exercise anywhere - in a restaurant, a park, a museum, on a bus or subway or in the lobby of a movie house.

Getting ready to get ready is a living process a daily process, and a vitally important part of it is to observe how people behave when the

77

are BEING. Most actors learn to act from watching other actors act on television and in films and so they become imitative of bad acting habits. BEING is a foreign state to them. Watching an actor on stage in a workshop scene and then observing him afterwards listening to the criticism - the difference is incredible. When he's listening and responding, just BEING, he is filled with emotional colors and contrasts and unpredictable fleeting thoughts that cross his face. We don't know what he's going to do, because he doesn't. His life has all the dimensions of reality.

There are many reasons for practicing observation exercises. It trains you to get involved more objectively in things outside of yourself instead of being limited by your own subjective concerns. It stretches your perception, which increases your affectability; the more you perceive, the more you respond to. As you develop skill in observation, you will learn to isolate elements of human behavior and define their origins so that later, on stage, you can create stimuli that will produce similar behavior in you. This exercise can be used as a means of getting an external sense of another person as a tool for characterization. It's important for you to observe and understand all kinds of human behavior and idiosyncrasies, because you have to deal with all levels and facets of behavior in your work.

There are specific things you look for when you are observing people. These are the categories of observation:

a.) How is the Person Dressed?
      How he's dressed has a lot to do with what
      that person's all about. The style, the
      apparent cost of the clothes, comfort or
      discomfort, color coordination, the concern

78

At the Farmers Market — "It's important for you to observe and understand all kinds of human behavior".

or lack of concern with his own clothing, whether it's in or out of style, etc. The person may be a millionaire wearing blue jeans that day. You take that chance. Fortunately, it isn't the only thing you see and you cross-reference with other observations.

b.) Props
What do people have protruding from their pockets? What is he holding onto? What is she carrying? What is he wearing in addition to the clothing - jewelry, a hat, pipe, cigarette holder. A man who has a plastic-lined pocket in his shirt filled with six pencils obviously does something with pencils. He has that liner there to protect his shirt. Now if he's wearing a suit, he does something with pencils that work clothes don't go with. Possibly some kind of clerical blue-collar position. A person with a briefcase might be moving around from place to place. The books people carry tell you a lot about their tasts in literature or about their work. Also observe the way people relate to their "props". Are they careful with them? Or careless? How do they open their car doors? Are they worried about the paint?

c.) Involvements and Relationships
Suppose a person is totally involved in what he's doing to the exclusion of everything around him. Is he doing this protectively to keep from having to deal with other people and things around him? Or is he more interested in what he's doing than in his environment? Or is he so involved with himself that he's unaware of the surroundings? Or is he under

81

pressure of some kind? Is he late? What
are the specifics that suggest a person's
involvement? You might be able to tell
whether a man is out to lunch with his
secretary by the way he relates to her.
Is he coming on to her sexually or are
they just talking business? Is he concerned with being seen by anybody? Is
he married or not? You can tell if people have been intimate with each other
by the way they relate. You can almost
tell at what point in a relationship two
people are by observing how they relate
to each other. Are they at the beginning
of a romantic relationship or at the end?
You can almost guess how many times they'
ve been intimate with each other. You
may be wrong, but that's okay. Keep on
observing and deducing.

d.) Awareness or the Lack of It
How does the person relate to his own
body? How aware is he of his own physi-
cality? How unaware? A person who is
a physical culturist, a weight-lifter,
relates to his body in a way that calls
attention to it. A woman who reached
pubescence too soon and hated her large
breasts may still be hunched over, trying
to hide them.

How do people relate to the weather? Do
they seem aware of what kind of day it
is? Are they aware of the other people
around them? Of the place? Some people
function no further than six inches away
from their faces and don't get involved
with things that demand a response.

e.) Compensations and Redirections
Compensation is a behavior which is super
imposed over what you really feel. It's

subtle thing that clings to a person
like a constant behavioral veil. For
example, a lady customer at a counter
is given the wrong change and politely
accepts it and walks away. Or she
quietly asks for the correct change,
please, and the salesperson yells, "Will
you wait a minute, I only got two hands!"
The customer smiles and says pleasantly,
"Alright." That's compensation. You
know she's not feeling alright at all.
She's feeling something else. Or another example, someone walks into a party
and is tense and self-conscious, but
compensates by being limp-wristed and
"super-relaxed".

Redirection is feeling one thing and
putting it into another more socially
acceptable area. For instance, someone
who feels like crying might laugh instead, because the thought of shedding
a tear is shameful. You can tell that
the laughter is not pure. It's redirection and belies the reality. If you
train yourself to observe, you'll see
the underlying truths. Many characters
in plays behave compensationally. These
observations help you to understand the
complexity of these behaviors and later
to create them.

f.) Self-Consciousness
The quickest way to spot people's sensitivities, the things they're anxious
about, is to watch how they point to it
like beacons in the night. The short
guy accentuates his shortness by standing
up to his full height so that he calls
attention to his size. The very tall,
lanky guy who slumps also calls attention
to his own concern about his height.

People who are embarassed about their
teeth often talk behind their hand or
keep the top lip stiff so you can't see
their teeth. A woman who had teen-age
acne and now has a face that is pocked
with scars never moves her face at all
as she talks to you. The immobility,
which she believes is concealing, only
rivets your eyes to her face. You, the
observer, can become expert in identifying self-consciousness and the various
ways people attempt to handle it.

g.) Eating and Other Activities
How someone relates to food reveals to
you whether eating is a big moment in his
day or not. Some people eat as if it wer
the entire consummation of life. You can
observe someone eating lunch as if he had
prepared for this moment yesterday. Another might always leave something on her
plate because a southern lady never clean
her plate. You can tell if someone had a
weight problem by the way he relates to
food even though he's not fat. It's all
deductive observation which is seeing how
people do what they do and then deducing
the reasons for it. To keep from falling
into the trap of script-writing, continu-
ally ask yourself, "What tells me that?"

h.) Time-Capsule
This observation can spread over all the
categories. The way a person dresses,
eats, relates to things around him, might
be walking out of a 1947 calendar or a
1950 movie magazine. This was probably
the most exciting time of life for him
and nothing that followed equalled it.
This is the point where his curiosity
died and the striving to grow ended.
Look for evidence of this in hair and

clothing style, colloquialisms, slang
of another era, sexual morality, and
nostalgic stories.

Your deductions might seem outrageously
unfounded. But encourage yourself to
wonder, ask, imagine and conclude. Take
chances. If you're wrong, fine. You're
strengthening your curiosity and adven-
turousness on and off the stage so that
in searching for a character in a play,
you'll be more likely to come up with
fresh, unconventional, but entirely human discoveries.

Purposes of the Farmers' Market Exercise:

- To increase your perception of behavior, its origins, its variety and
  peculiarities.

- To make you aware of where, how, and
  why people behave.

- To increase your affectability.

- To give you a barometer of your own
  behavior in terms of its authenticity,
  because you have a life model.

- To help you understand and create behavior that isn't your own, to help
  you get a sense of other people.

What are realities? How do you create
realities? You create the source, not
the manifestation.

Do it everyday.

Sensory Awareness

Discovering your senses and how they work is
an essential aspect of getting ready to get
ready. We will go deeply into sense memory,
but for now, let's start with discovering the
senses. Your five senses are your doors of
perception. Through these doors comes everything that has ever affected you and you are
the sum total of all these things. Knowing
how each of your senses works, individually
and personally, opens your doors wider and
teaches you to use your senses in a creative
process.

Your five senses are:

1. Visual
    Everything you see. Seeing.

2. Tactile
    Feeling, touching, everything that comes
    into contact with your skin.

3. Auditory
    Hearing.

4. Olfactory
    Smelling.

5. Gustatory
    Tasting.

5½. Kinesthetic
    A muscular response to real and imaginary
    objects. It's part of the tactile area,
    but it's deeper than just an epidermal
    response. Blind people develop this part
    of their sensory equipment much more fully
    than people who see. In class I discov-
    ered the importance of the fifth and a hal

sense by putting two actors with their
backs to each other about six inches
apart and told them to communicate without touch, sound or sight. I found out
that people could feel not only the presence of another person, but also that
person's physical and emotional attitude.
It's elusive, but it can be perceived.
Sitting in a movie theatre you feel the
presence of someone behind you and when
that person leaves you feel the absence.
It's your kinesthetic response to something there that was not there before
or is not there now.

23. Sensory Inventory: How the Senses Work

Long before I ever thought of teaching acting
I studied with someone who introduced me to
sense memory and I began an intense exploration of it on my own. I worked with my senses
for hours every day. I really had to find out
how my senses functioned, why they would respond to a certain thing. How do I know that
cold is cold and not hot, or blue? What tells
me that?

I became quite a fanatic about it because my
search was so exciting and engrossing. The
phenomenal thing about sense memory is when it
starts to work for you, when you start to feel,
really feel the heat of an imaginary flame,
when you start to sweat in a cold room or get
gooseflesh in a hot room. You feel unique,
elite, one of the chosen few.

First of all, I isolated each sense and concen-
trated on one at a time. I'd try to find out
where on my hand I felt anything and why I felt
more in some parts of my hand than in others.
I'd take the end of a pencil and run it slowly
down the inside of my hand from the tip of my

fingers to my wrist and I'd find that at the
very tip of my finger, just below the finger-
nail, I didn't feel as much as on the pad of
my finger. I concluded there must be more
nerve endings in the pad than on the tip. I
also discovered the finger pads are more sensitive than the second joint of each finger.
I'd take a matchbook or coffee cup or whatever object I was working with and explore the
insides of my fingers with it, moving it to
the back of my hand, touching it to my cheek,
up the arm and all over the rest of my body.
I found out many things, such as that the
parts of me usually covered with clothing
were more sensitive to temperature and texture than the exposed parts. Holding an ice
cube in each hand, I'd explore how long it
took for the cold to numb my sense. I'd take
off my shoes and walk around barefoot feeling
the differences between the rug and the tile
floor and I'd attempt to relate to objects
with my feet as I usually did with my hands,
picking things up off the floor.

Then I might go to my nose and investigate my
sense of smell. I'd fill a tabletop with a
variety of odors - a perfume, a chocolate bar,
a lemon, sachets, can of coffee. I found that
by sniffing deeper, throwing the odors back
into my nose the way a dog does, I smelled mor
fully and more kinds of odors. I decided that
an odor must be the molecules of the object
floating in the air and getting up into the
nose to be interpreted by the brain. I'd ask
myself questions. Where is smell taking place
in my nose? Where exactly do I smell? Which
nostril do I get the most response from? I'd
cover one nostril and then the other. I realized that the olfactory sense gets saturated
very quickly. There'd come a point where I
couldn't smell any of the objects on the table
and I'd have to walk away for awhile. Then

I'd come back and try to define the specific
parts of each odor and exactly where in my
nose I smelled it.

In tasting, I found that I taste with the
roof of my mouth as well as the sides, the
top and the tip of my tongue and in the
cheeks. I've talked to people who've gotten
dentures which cover up the roof of the
mouth and they tell me they lose a portion
of their taste and have to learn to compen-
sate with the other parts of their mouth.

I found that in my mouth I taste a great deal
on the sides of my tongue so that in rolling
things around, such as a piece of hard candy,
I'd experience bursts of flavor when it got
to certain parts of my mouth. Then I'd try
it with coffee with cream and sugar in it.
I'd roll the coffee around and when I'd get
to the same section, the sides of my tongue
and under my tongue, there'd be bursts of
flavor. I'd suck in air while I had liquid
in my mouth, as wine-tasters do, and the air,
mixed with the liquid, for some reason en-
hanced the taste. Maybe the air excited the
receptors, the taste buds. I think I even
taste with my gums. I'm not sure of that,
but I know my teeth _feel_. You can take a
pencil and put it between your top and bottom teeth and you can feel textures and shapes.
For years that's how people found out if a
pearl was real or fake. The real pearl has
little irregular bumps on it that are perceived by the teeth. Of course, with any
object in my mouth I'd always be aware of
temperature and texture even though I was
concentrating on the sense of taste and not
the tactile sense.

Visually, my eyes were attracted to what interested them at first - colors, shapes,

sizes. The eye skips over many details of an object. The visual sense has a tendency to take a lot for granted and unless we train it to be specific, it just takes in the overall object. When I'd focus on something and then look away, I'd experience an after-image like the negative of a photo. I worked with each eye individually and found differences and peculiarities of each one. I explored dimension by holding up my finger in front of my face and quickly blinked one eye and then the other. I'd look at the texture of an object and then touch it and check out the difference between what my eyes told me the texture was and what my tactile sense told me. My eyes investigated the depth of objects and the distances between them. I'd blind myself momentarily with a bright light, and then find out how long it took for my sight to return.

I really enjoyed playing with my ears. Ears are shaped conically to trap sound. People whose ears stick out from the head hear better, so I'd point my ear in certain directions and cup it with my hand and, like a radar cone I'd hear more of the subtleties. You get close to finding out how you sound to other people by cupping your ears and talking. I'd turn a piece of music on very loud and then very low and move my head in various directions trying to find out at what point I was the most sensitive. I tried to break down sounds into vibrations to learn how I hear and to find out what hearing is. Sounds that come directly in front of you or in back of yo are hard to determine in terms of their direction, their origin. I'd plug up both ears jus to listen to the sounds of my own body and I discovered that my body is very noisy. I coul hear the coursing of my blood, the pounding of my heart, swallowing, breathing and digesting.

Finding out how your senses work is an exciting adventure. You will become your own pathfinder and the paths are infinite. The more you explore your sensory apparatus, the more totally you will be able to use it in the craft of acting.

24. Sensitizing

This exercise should be done daily. We do it at the beginning of each class, because it's an essential element of the actor's preparation. It enormously heightens your sensory availability.

It can be done in any position. As in the Sensory Inventory, the exercise requires the isolation of the senses. Start with the tactile sense, beginning with the top of your head, your scalp. It's as if you are living in your scalp. When your scalp begins to tingle or you feel a pulse there or the heat of your own body, it's an indication that that part is sensitized. Then you move to your forehead, your face, your chin. Move down your body in four inch sections until you get to the soles of your feet, living each section until you feel it is sensitized.

Then go to your ears. Without touching them with your hands, become aware of their structure. Then, as you did in the tactile area, live in your ears. Listen to every sound from the most obvious to the most subtle, their directions and origins, all the way down to the component parts of silence.

Then the nose. Become aware of its structure without touching it, the apertures, the mucous membrane, the inner nose. Live in your nose. Become aware of all the odors around

you. Try to smell all of them and the element
of each one. It's as if you've become a giant
nose.

Then to the mouth. Focus on it, the gums, the
teeth, tongue, cheeks. Taste the tastes in
your own mouth. You might have some toothpast
left over from brushing your teeth. You might
have a coffee taste or the aftertaste of a
sandwich. Do it until you taste even the tast
of your own flesh.

You can sensitize your eyes in one of two ways
Isolate a small area, maybe the corner of a ta
ble top, and, by living in your eyes, attempt
to see every minute detail. Or look at an object, a small portion of it, and then look awa
and try to visualize that same portion. Then
look back and go to another portion and repeat
the same process, living in your eyes.

The entire exercise might take you fifteen min
utes, or twenty, when you first do it, but as
you practice it over a period of time, you con
dition your senses to respond instantly and yo
can do it all in less than two minutes.

Getting to the Deeper Self

After becoming aware of how you feel and what'
around you, it's important to reach down more
deeply into yourself and begin finding a fulle
relationship to who you are, what you feel, wh
you want, what you experience. You are as individual as your fingerprints and the unique
contribution of that individuality is dependen
on your getting to know all that is there and
using it in your work. The following exercise
are designed to help you get to your deeper
self.

25. Stream of Consciousness

This is the verbalization of everything that
you're thinking and feeling without the emphasis, as in Personal Inventory, on finding
out how you feel. It establishes a moment-
to-moment flow of everything that is going
on. Doing this exercise regularly enables
you to express everything without obstruc-
tion and frees all the impulses that go on
underneath the level of life on which we
usually live. It's an antidote to the habit
of functioning above your real self.

26. I'm Afraid That. . .

A verbal stream in which each sentence begins
with "I'm afraid that. . .". For example,
"I'm afraid my agent is no good and I'll
never work again. I'm afraid I'll get old
and die alone. I'm afraid I won't succeed
on the level I want, won't get recognition
for what I know I am. I'm afraid of being
poor. I'm afraid to go to that party tonight,
all those people I don't know. I'm afraid to
be afraid. I'm afraid people will know I'm
afraid. I'm afraid my kid will grow up and be
a bum. I'm afraid of falling in love." And
on and on and on.

The value of this exercise is to put you in
touch with your fears which you often hide
from yourself. By exposing the fears, they
become less crippling. And getting to know
and express your fears is another step in
the process of knowing yourself.

27. I Like That. . .

The positive twin to "I'm Afraid That. . ."
"I like that I'm alive today. I like that
I'm brushing my dog's fur. I like having

breakfast in bed. I like that I worked out at
the gym today. I'm excited about going out
tonight. . ." Here also you'll surprise yourself sometimes and find out likes you didn't
know you had. It's also a good exercise for
picking up your spirits.

28. I Care, I Don't Care

Another type of verbal stream, emphasizing
what you care about and what you don't care
about. Express your caring and non-caring
about everything from worldly issues to the
most trivial objects around you.

29. Personal Point of View

There are two ways to do this exercise - either
to yourself and for yourself, or out loud in
front of other people. Both ways help you to
find out what your personal point of view is
about anything; something you may not have
known you had a point of view about at all.
Saying it in front of others develops your
courage to expose and take responsibility for
what you feel.

30. Center Circle

Any of these exercises can be done standing in
the center of a circle of people and when done
this way, each exercise takes on the added dimension of being on the spot.

Center Circle is also an exercise unto itself,
the forerunner of Dealing With the Demon. In
the center of the circle, you become aware of
what being on the spot does to you, physically
and emotionally. In verbally acknowledging
that, you learn more about what affects you in
that situation and how. The expression of how
you feel frees you to function more comfortably

94

31. Personal Inventory

This exercise, already described in Chapter I, is an extremely important one in getting to the self. Add the question, "What do I want?" to "How do I feel?"

32. Self Inventory

Joan: Eric, is Self Inventory anything like Personal Inventory?

Eric: No, no, not at all. Self Inventory is a process of taking stock of your life - your day, the last month, the last year, five years ago and so on. It's a recalling of emotional events in your life and other kinds of experiences, but most important, it's the cataloguing of the sensory elements of those experiences so that when you need those feelings later on in your work, you know the buttons to push. You've got the means to restimulate yourself.

Joan: I think I know what you mean. I do that a lot, mostly when I go to bed at night.

Eric: Yes, that's when I do it too. Actually it started when I was a boy and I used to hate to go to bed at night. I used to have to con myself into going to sleep. So I'd get in bed and make up stories, aggrandize myself, fantasize occurrences, be a famous actor with people applauding me. This is how I started to act, really. Then later on, in later years, when I was studying acting and having difficulty laying my hands on choices, I would go to bed at

95

night and I would start to go over my day. What happened today? What was significant? Who did I see? I'd reconstruct the day sensorily, so to speak, without doing a sense memory exercise.

I went over the current day every night for about a month. Then for the next month or two I went back a week and picked a day out of that week and reconstructed it. After I could do that, I went back a whole month. And then I'd go back five or six months at random. I'd let my mind wander and say, "Okay, think of an experience, an important experience related to an important day. . . Okay, my birthday, November 19th. . . Okay, now I'm at November 19th. . . Did anything happen toward the beginning of the month? Yeah, I can remember something. . . Okay, what about something after my birthday, something toward the end of the month?" In other words, I'd use my birthday or any meaningful day as a center point from which to work backwards and forwards. As I did Self Inventory, I found I could recall more and more going all the way back to the age of four and five and really remember smelling and tasting and hearing and feeling things. And I could really use those things now. They were usable to me as an actor.

Joan: That's fabulous. But you know most people have difficulty remembering.

Eric: Oh, sure. Particularly after five years. It's vague and general.

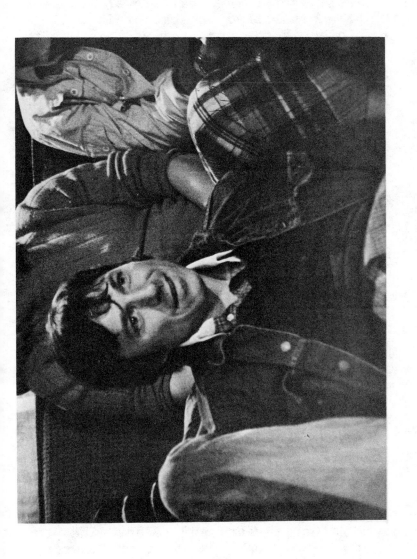

Greg Mulavey doing "self inventory" exercise in class.

Joan: That's right. People say to me, Joan how do you remember all that! That happened so long ago!

Eric: Well, everything that's ever happened to us is locked in some brain cell, stored in the unconscious. We don't ever forget anything.

Joan: I found that out in psychoanalysis. One of the things analysis did for me, not to mention all of the things it didn't do for me, was it opened up my memory. I re-experienced very early events in my life and these events are purely sensory, Eric, because that's before you know any words.

Eric: I never could remember my childhood. I mean really, not past a certain point. I couldn't remember below ten except fragmentary images - my father walking through the door lifting me up - my mother dressing me for school. But they were fleeting images. Until I started doing Self Inventory and stretched my memory. I made up the exercise to help myself as an actor and then later when I began teaching, I discovered a lot of actors need it.

Joan: You said you kept a journal too.

Eric: Yes, I did, for awhile. And that's another way you can do Self Inventory. There are two ways, really. The way I described, going back a day or a month or a year, and so on. And you can also keep a daily journal, writing down significant experiences of that day. You record not only the events, but also the sensory stimuli so that a year or two or three years from now you can look back in your journal to May 14th or May 15th and you have right there the whole experience - how you felt and all the sensory elements that made you feel that way.

Joan: I've kept a journal from time to time, but when I first started studying with you, you told me not to write anything down.

Eric: Because you were writing things down instead of learning them organically, but now you've grown beyond that. It's always a danger when actors put things in writing because they tend to feel it's been accomplished. They think they've done the work on it. But actually they haven't done the work on it. It's just the raw material.

Joan: I really understand that now. Listen, Eric, there's something I want to ask you. You know that romantic idealism we're looking for in the Swan Lake section of my play? I've been searching in various areas of my life and I think I've found something. It's the three summers I spent at Four Winds Camp when I was in my early teens. They were idyllic summers. See, look at this list here. These are the sensory frag- ments - my middy uniform, it was always starched and it had a certain smell to it. The various cabins that I stayed in. The balcony of the lodge at night and the feeling of girls' arms around my waist when we used to sing a good- night song to each other. Roman Meal cereal, that crunchy texture. And the

smells of pine and balsam and dough-
nuts frying.

Eric: These are all things you remembered
from that time?

Joan: Yes.

Eric: How did you feel overall at that time,
the most specific memories of how you
felt? What were they?

Joan: I felt so full of hope and joy and romance. It was, I think, the last time
in my life that I felt so purely opti-
mistic about everything.

Eric: All three summers?

Joan: All three summers. Particularly the
last summer when they crowned my Gypsy
Princess. It was sort of like the
validation of this belief that life
was joyful.

Eric: Now in that section of your play you
want to feel hope and joy and romantic
idealism.

Joan: And at the same time a kind of sadness
because it isn't there anymore. I want
to stimulate the feelings of hope and
joy and then realize that they're gone.

Eric: Okay. Now, using the Self Inventory,
go back over your list of sensory stimuli - the middy uniform, the lodge at
night and so on, and what you might do
is first get an overall sense of how
these things make you feel. Then if
they seem to be taking you in the right
direction, select one of them and work

sensorily on a more specific level and
see if it takes you where you want to
go. You may find some even more poignant elements than what's on your list,
but it all starts with the Self Inventory.

Joan: Eric, what I might try is in that Swan
Lake section, when I'm in the doctor's
office. I might work for being in the
pine woods at Four Winds, wildflowers
all around, the sun and the air - I
remember the air had a mixture of chill
and hot. It was like wine on my skin
and I could surround myself in the doctor's office with this sensory element
of that past time. . .

Eric: And the fact that you are no longer in
your teens and you're not in that place
should stimulate the sadness you want
in the scene.

Joan: Yes, I think it will.

Eric: One thing I want to add to that, caution
you about. What makes it there and then
specifically at that time? Was it a
particular smell only indigenous to
there? Was it a particular feeling
related only to that place, to that
time? Otherwise, it may be a conglomeration of many experiences. It has
to be specified. Taking Self Inventory,
dealing with sensory elements, you must
specify what makes it that particular
thing.

Joan: Because a conglomerate thing is general.
Right?

Eric: Right. What you want is the purity of

a specific response.

Getting Related to People
On and Off the Stage

Since acting usually takes place in a situation between two or more people, a vital part of Getting Ready to Get Ready is learning how to relate to people and overcoming the obstacles that prevent you from relating freely. The exercises in this section all deal with relationship, either between two people or between an individual and a group. These exercises are neither busy work for beginning actors nor idle gymnastics to keep yourself limber between jobs. On the contrary, they apply directly to the craft of acting and are most effective when done "under fire" - that is, in actual rehearsals of plays or on a movie set.

Among professional actors there is a stigma attached to doing "exercises" on the job. So-called "pros" frown on bringing the classroom to the set and the serious actor has to hide behind scenery to do his preparations. This attitude is part of a tradition of slick professionalism and cool, impersonal acting. But art is totally personal and rehearsals should be designed to reveal and enhance each artist's unique contribution to the material.

You can't deny your feelings in life and then turn a switch when you get on stage and magically become a free, colorfully expressive actor. As we've said before and will say again, the approach is far more than a way for work. It's a way of life. It has to be, otherwise it won't work for you when you get on stage. If directors would lead their casts

through some of these exercises, if they would
dare to ruffle some of the feathers, they would
get results in their final products that would
far outstrip the cardboard cutouts we now see
in theatre. Audiences would begin to see the
difference between reality and imitation and
actors would begin to demand their right to use
rehearsal time creatively to encourage the infinite variety of life that comes out of BEING.
Instead, what usually goes on in rehearsals are
the social amenities and the niceties. All
this social concern prevents people from ex-
ploring their inner lives, which is where the
gold is.

The Round Exercises

There are a number of Rounds with several different emphases, but all of the Rounds are done
with the people sitting in a circle so that
everyone can see everyone else. The Rounds
originated in class where they've been used
for eight years with impressive results, but
they can also be used in a rehearsal group.

Actors in scenes often relate to each other
generally, fearing really to affect each other.
The Round demands a greater degree of honesty
in relating; more specific exposure of what
you really feel without hiding behind a character. You are only speaking for you. Over a
period of time, as you practice the Rounds, you
become more specific and personal and that carries into your acting. The Rounds help you
eliminate the separation between you and the
character.

The basic purpose of these Round exercises is
to stimulate relationship on an honest, organic, one-to-one, one-to-three, one-to-eight

level. Another purpose is to get to know
yourself better through the eyes of others.
Also you learn to overcome your social re-
luctance and the fear of expressing so-
called negative emotions. You allow yourself to experience conflict with other people, which is inherent in most dramatic
material but which our conditioning teaches
us to avoid. By taking responsibility for
all that you feel, you get deeper into your
inner life.

I've found that, in class, the Rounds produce love, affection and concern among the
actors and I'm convinced the same thing
would happen in a rehearsal group.

33. Ego Reconstruction

Sitting in a circle, observe and perceive
the people around you. Whether it's your
first time in the group or whether you know
the people well, express to individuals your
perceptions of them in a way that you feel
would be constructive or helpful to their
growth. For example: "You know, Sandra, I
get the feeling that you don't really listen
to what people say to you. . . Joe, in the
last couple of weeks you seem so open and
warm, it's a pleasure to look at you. . .",
etc.

Be careful to avoid two-way conversations or
it degenerates into a coffee klatch. It's
easy to lose control of this exercise. Whether or not you agree or disagree with what's
said to you, just listen.

Naturally, there will be a degree of subjec-
tivity and bias in what's said. Some women
are prettier than others, some actors work
more than others and there's jealousy. But

105

for the most part, people are surprisingly affirmative in this exercise. And if the actor hears the same kind of things said to him over a period of time, he begins to accept that what has been said to him is valid. If a pretty but mousey actress hears often enough that she is pretty, she may soon accept that as a reality.

The exercise is as beneficial for the person expressing the observation as it is to the one hearing it.

When we do it in class, I impose two limitations: you may not be cruel for the sake of being cruel. And you may not violate anybody's privacy without permission. The leader of the Round is responsible for enforcing these rules.

34. Reluctancy

The word is neither correct nor a typographical error. Over the years I've coined words and made up words that have special meaning to me and my students because they communicate what I want to say better than the right word.

A Reluctancy is the expression of anything you feel uncomfortable about, anything that's difficult for you to say publicly, things you feel ashamed of, afraid of, uptight about or reluctant to express for any reason. The exercise is done in the round and for the sake of guidelines, we've used the following categories: Self, Encounter, Physical and Sexual. There are many other areas you can use. These categories should not restrict you. Any kind of reluctancy is right for the exercise.

Self-Reluctancy is the expression of anything that is about you. "I am reluctant to open my mouth. . . I'm reluctant to say anything. . .

I feel I'm going to make an ass out of myself. . . I'm ashamed to admit that I wish
I weren't a mother, I wish my children were
gone and I could be free. . ."

Encounter Reluctancy is anything you feel
reticent about saying to another person in
the room. "I'm really very attracted to you,
Mary. How do you feel about me. . ?" (Mary
shouldn't answer at this point, because two-
way conversations disintegrate the exercise)
. . . "Karl, you hurt my feelings when you
walked in the room tonight and passed right
by me without saying anything. . . Pete, I'm
sick of your whining. If you really want
what you say you want, get up off your ass
and go get it. . ."

Physical Reluctancy is the exposure of anything about your body that concerns you or
anything you are physically reluctant to do.
For instance, you might feel proud of your
physique, but reluctant to get up and take
off your shirt and flex your muscles. In
this exercise you would encourage yourself
to do it. Or you might feel that you're
overweight and you have a fat belly that
you're ashamed of and so you'd get up and
expose it and talk about how it affects you.
Or you might want to touch someone, but feel
afraid of their response. In this exercise
you would carry out that action. (The only
limitation here is against violating another
person's rights. You're not allowed to as-
sault someone sexually or hurt anyone.)

Sexual Reluctancy is anything sexual you feel
reluctant to express. For example, in one
class a student said he was very uptight
about the size of his penis. He said it's
about five and a half inches and he wished it
were bigger. . . Rosemary admitted she fakes

orgasms. . . Others have expressed fear of
first sexual encounters, anxiety about being
able to get and maintain an erection.

Reluctancy is a training exercise. It should
not be used in a casual rehearsal group. The
exercise can be dangerous unless it is led by
a skillful and responsible leader in a group
where the people meet regularly. When it works
well, it is exciting, sometimes explosive, often funny and always freeing. If you do this
exercise over a period of time, it progressively opens more doors of expression. The inhibitions you started with disappear and this freedom carries directly into your acting. The
more you expose yourself in Reluctancy and in
your life, the more areas are open to you on
the stage and the more personal your expression in a piece of material. Reluctancy teaches
you that you need not fear the skeletons in
your closet. Everybody has them and it's okay.
Many actors are free in some areas, but totally
closed in others. Reluctancy is designed to
open all your doors. It encourages you to relate to other people very personally from the
center of your own being, and your relationships on stage are honest and real. The fear
that what you feel and express on stage will
be taken personally, and yourself held responsible for it, stops most actors. They hide
behind the lines and the character and if it
gets hot, they cop out by saying, "That isn't
me. That's the character." There is only you.
There is no character. The character is you.

35. How I See Myself

This exercise is also done in the round, but it
is done individually. The person doing the
exercise is either called on by the leader, or
volunteers to do it. You need not get up and
stand in the center, because the exercise is

"spot"-producing enough as it is. In anywhere from two minutes to ten, talk about
how you see yourself and think of yourself.
Not the way you think other people perceive
you, but the way you feel you are. The trap
to avoid in the exercise is the second-guessing of what other people might think of you.
Stay true to your self image.

For instance, "I see myself as being very intelligent. When people meet me for the first
time, I can see immediately that they know
I'm intelligent. I'm articulate. I think a
lot, I think an awful lot. I feel I'm pretty
attractive. I think I'm very attractive.
I've got a groovy body, I've got a good personality and when I get excited, I feel I'm
a very exciting person. I feel I'm sexually
attractive and women relate to me very well
and I'm talented, far more talented than I've
ever to this point been able to release. I
like people. I like to relate to people.
I'm good at that. I feel I'm moody sometimes.
I get depressed and very low, and when I'm
like that I often alienate people. . ."

Try to cover all facets of yourself. When
you're finished, ask for feedback from the
group. Say to them, *Is the way I see myself
consistent or inconsistent with the way you
see me?"* The feedback can come from as many
as seven or eight people depending on time.
In my two-day marathons, I allow all those
who want to give feedback to give it, no matter how long it takes.

In giving feedback, a person might say, "Yeah,
I think you're intelligent and I think you
think a lot, but I don't feel you're expressive of what you think. . . I would like to
hear more of what you think. You think too
much.

Someone else might say, "I agree that you're sexually attractive, but you withhold it. To me you come across cold."

Sometimes a person's self-image is delusional, totally based on fantasy. Feedback from the group makes him aware of the gap between his self-image and the reality.

Everyone doing the Self Image will receive enough responses to make a valid cross-reference of what is true. The exercise is invaluable for dealing with the inconsistencies between what you think you are and what you actually are. You might be everything you think you are, but very little of it is being expressed. You may feel that your relationships to people on and off the stage are very full and free, but in fact you may learn in the exercise that this isn't true. The feedback will direct you specifically to areas that you need work in.

36. Feedback

Although feedback is used in Self Image, this exercise is separate from it. Again it's done in the round and also on an individual basis, but this time it's strictly voluntary. If you want Feedback, you ask for it. There are two ways you can do it. The first way is based on George Bach's mindreading exercise and goes something like this: "Joe, I think you think I'm abstract and complicated and don't understand what I'm talking about and I become mystical and abstract to hide the truth, which is that I really don't know what I'm talking about. Is that what you think?"

Then Joe answers you, and he might say, "I never thought any of that. I don't know where you got that." Or he might say, "Yeah, I think you are very complicated and I think

110

you do make things more difficult to understand than they have to be, but it isn't
because I think you don't know what you're
talking about."

Now the second kind is when you ask a person
for feedback in a specific area. "Joan, what
do you think of me as a teacher? Do you
think I'm patient and understanding with
people?" And Joan might say, "Yes, I think
you're very patient." Or she might say, "No,
I think you could be more patient with some
people."

You might ask, "Sue, what do you think of me
as an actor?" And Sue might answer, "What
do you mean what do I think of you as an actor? Do you mean do I think you're talented,
or do I think you're a particular kind of
actor, or do you need work in certain areas?"
The person being asked for feedback can demand more specificity. Then you might ask
Sue, "Okay, what do you think of my work recently? Do you think I've grown as an actor?"
Now that's specific. And Sue could answer,
"The last two scenes I've seen you do - I've
seen a great deal of growth. You're simpler.
You're more related to the other actor. You'
re much less tense."

When you volunteer for this exercise, you can
use either or both of these approaches. Feedback is designed to help you understand yourself better, to know if what you're perceiving is true, and also - vitally important -
the exercise encourages you to reach out to
people and ask for response to you.

This kind of round is suitable for a rehearsal
group, because it can flush out those negative
mindreadings that occur in rehearsals and im-
pede the creative work. For example, the

111

actor who thinks the director hates him, or
the director who thinks the actors are laughing at him behind his back. An aspect that
makes it good for a rehearsal group is that
it's self-regulatory. You don't have to ask
for feedback if you don't want it.

Two People Relationship Exercises

These exercises can be used in a variety of
situations - classroom, rehearsal group, private rehearsal between you and another actor,
on a motion picture set - anywhere. They are
all designed to get you related to another
person, to get you *involved, related and responsive to another person.* Besides this cen-
tral purpose, these exercises have additional
benefits:

- To help your concentration.

- To alleviate your tension.

- To stimulate your vulnerability.

- To get you to be more personal.

- To pique your curiosity.

- To elevate your ability to perceive and observe.

- To increase your courage by asking for what
  you want.

- To overcome physical inhibitions to touching
  another person.

- To sensitize you to the other person and what's
  going on with him.

112

- To train you to look <u>into</u> another person
rather than <u>at</u> him.

37. Hold Hands and Look at Each Other

Best results when done for a long period of
time, at least fifteen minutes. Two people
sit and hold each other's hands comfortably
and look into each other's eyes. Allow and
encourage everything that happens to happen.
At first, you might be embarrassed and want
to look away. You might want to talk, which
isn't allowed. As you continue the exercise,
many feelings are expressed between you. At
the end of the time, a relationship has begun
which can go in any direction.

38. Two People Touch

Can be done with your eyes open or closed.
No talking. Simply relate to each other by
touching and feeling. You will become emotionally related as well as physically.

39. Relate As If for the First Time

A good exercise when two actors have known
each other a long time and have begun taking
things for granted. Approach the exercise
by first looking at your partner as if you've
never seen him or her before. Actually search
for things which you have honestly never noticed before. Use all of your senses together
in the same way, discovering things you've
never been aware of. Talking is allowed if
you feel like it. Really listen for sounds
and intonations that are new to you. This
emphasis will stimulate a kind of first-time
relationship and will freshen your rehearsal
with many new facets of behavior and responses
Instead of taking each other for granted, you
will become unpredictable to each other and

eventually to an audience.

40. Ask For What You Want

A two-people exercise which can also be done
in a group. As it says in the title, that's
what you do. You ask the other person for
what you want from him or her. The success
of the exercise depends on how courageous you
are in really exposing your needs. The trap
here is to make smalltalk - "What did you do
today?". . . I want to know what you did before you came here. . ." Instead of really
asking for what you want. . . "Do you like
me?. . . How do you feel about me?. . . I
wish we could be closer than we are. . . I
want you to be more sensitive to my feelings."

The other person can reply if he wishes, or
choose not to. Each person does it until
he's finished asking for everything he wants.
Then the other person does it.

41. Double Exposure

This is an exercise designed to get two people
related personally, as all the exercises in
this part of the chapter are meant to do.
Double Exposure helps you relate to the other
person personally. That word can't be stressed
too much. Personally. It is done either standing or sitting. Look at each other and progressively expose more personal things about yourself to the other actor. The actors take turns
speaking and listening. It should not be a
dialogue. Two-way conversation is discouraged,
although you can ask each other for clarifica-
tion if you don't understand something. Start
simply and become more personal with each exposure. Don't violate your privacy or anybody
else's. There is a definite line between what
is personal and what is private. Don't expose

114

anything that can hurt you or anyone else
such as names, dates, places and facts that
can be incriminating in any way. The line
between what is private and what is personal
varies among individuals, but if your line
of what is private includes everything, then
you're not being personal!

42. Telepathy

Not an ESP exercise. It's called Telepathy
because it demands that two people communicate without words, pantomime, or charade-
type gestures. It encourages them to reach
deeply into each other to try to find out
what's going on. What is the other person
trying to communicate? You may never find
out what he's telling you, but the reaching
is what's important in Telepathy.

Sit or stand close enough to each other to
make physical contact. Start with your eyes
closed. Have an intent and try to communicate it to the other person through your body
and, at the same time, try to receive his
message. Holding hands, you can express a
lot to each other just by the energies flowing through, but it's important that you express yourself through all parts of your body.
After awhile, open your eyes and continue
giving and receiving impulses without words
or illustrative gestures. You may use non-
verbal sounds.

You'll find you'll be much more involved with
the other actor than before and less dependent
on words to express that involvement. Your
relationship will occur on subtler levels of
behavior and have more dimension than if you
had started with words. Telepathy is a good
exercise to start a rehearsal. The next logical step would be to begin working with the

choices you're using in the scene.

43.   Observe, Wonder and Perceive II

This is the two-people version. The exercise
has already been described in the section on
Awareness, but here it's used to stimulate relationship and not only to get you related to
the other actor, but to get you involved with
each other and ready to work. You can do it
in any physical position as long as you can
look at each other. Observe, perceive and wonder about the other actor. That means anything
that you see, hear, feel, taste or smell. You
will observe things that are obviously there -
"I observe that you're sitting down and putting
your hands in your lap." You'll perceive behind what is obviously there - a fleeting look
in the eye, a subtle gesture which might be
protective or defensive and you might deduce,
"I perceive from your behavior that you're
getting ready to do this exercise and you're
a little uncomfortable." Then you encourage
the things that you truly wonder about - "I
wonder if you're uncomfortable because of the
exercise or bacause of me." Mostly you'll
wonder about things that you perceive sensorily. You might feel the texture of the person's cashmere jacket and wonder if he's
wealthy. You might pick up a scent of cologne mixed with perspiration and wonder if
she put the cologne on without taking a bath,
or if she's just very nervous at the moment.

Allow your observations, perceptions and wonderments to be kicked off by all your five
senses and to go where they will:

"I wonder why he's so stiff. He really looks
uptight. He wears an awful lot of jewelry.
I wonder why. I hear an accent. I wonder
where he's from. He's kind of social and

Laurie Burton doing a "wonder, perceive and observe" with Dan

phony, all that politeness. I wonder what
he's really thinking and feeling. He doesn't
show anything. What would he do if I told
him I think he's phony? I just saw something
- he lost his cool for a minute. I saw fear
in his face. It even affected his voice,
there's a faint tremor there. . .", . . .
etc., etc.

You can do the exercise silently or semi-
audibly or out loud. The reason for doing it
semi-audibly is to take you out of your head
by verbalizing your responses so that you can
hear them, although your partner can't. The
advantage of doing it out loud is that it
stimulates a verbal relationship, an involvement that gets you out of yourself, off the
spot, and into each other. The only caution
is to avoid a gab session which would distract
you from rehearsing. Stay with your observations, perceptions and wonderments.

44. Two People BEING

This is a four-part exercise. I started using
it in class regularly to promote the state of
BEING. The exercise is preparation - getting
ready to work with another person, getting
ready to do a rehearsal, getting ready to do
a scene. Two people stand in front of a group,
either a rehearsal group or a class or in an
audition. It's important that the two people
doing the exercise remain standing throughout,
because it intensifies the feeling of being
on the spot.

In the first part, both actors express semi-
audibly in stream-of-consciousness style all
their anxieties and tensions about being in
front of the group, all their awareness of
what's going on. No one hears the actor, but
the actor hears himself. He must actually

say what he's thinking to avoid an inner head game. "I'm standing here and I see the people looking at me. They're all looking at me as if they expect something and that intimidates me. Joanne is staring at me and I feel she's hostile and it makes me uptight. Joe just walked out. Maybe I'm boring to him. I'm afraid of being dull. Gee, I have a lot of tension in the back of my neck. . . I feel better now. I still have some tension, but it's okay. I feel I could get involved with my partner."

Once you have acknowledged and "dealt with the demons", expurgated some of your tension and become more comfortable in relation to the audience, you go to the second part of the exercise, which is to Observe-Wonder-Perceive about your partner. Do this in the same way as described in the exercise above.

When you feel sufficiently involved with your partner, go to the third part. (Throughout the entire exercise you continue to acknowledge and express anything that intrudes upon your awareness, such as a creeping tension or people moving in the audience and your concern about that.) In the third part, work for a simple sensory choice in relation to your partner without obligating yourself to any result. We'll explain in detail later on how to work for a sensory choice. You might try to create eyeglasses on your partner or a mustache or different color hair or bad breath or a certain look in his eyes that doesn't now exist. The purpose here is to get you started on the sensory process and to prime you to take on an emotional obligation, as in a scene.

If you are using this exercise as preparation for doing a scene, now is the time you start working for your first choice in that scene.

And that's the fourth part. If you're using
it just as a BEING exercise, then in this
fourth part you obligate yourself to something you want to feel in relation to your
partner, such as jealousy, desire, compassion,
fear, etc. Make the obligation very clear to
yourself. It's not just general jealousy or
general fear. Make clear to yourself what
you're jealous about. Then make a sensory
choice that you think might stimulate that
particular kind of jealousy and work for it,
going wherever the choice takes you.

*The BEING exercise is designed to get you in
touch with who you are, what you feel, how
you're functioning in terms of here and now.
That reality is the only place you can act
from. There isn't any other place you can
act from organically.*

45. Rock and Stroke

Two people sit on the floor. One person crad-
les the other in his lap, as you might do
with a small child, and rocks him gently,
petting and stroking and possibly humming a
lullaby. Both people should totally give
themselves to this exercise, which is non-
verbal. After five or ten minutes, the rock-
er becomes the rockee and vice versa. It is
not a sexual exercise. Men can do it with
men and women with women.

The visible results of this exercise are
startling. People really change during that
time. They become mellow, soft, open, warm
and loving. The exercise pushes some kind
of primal button, the basic need to be held
and stroked. It's a marvelous exercise for
starting a rehearsal or ending a rehearsal,
for starting or ending a class.

Getting Ready to Get Ready is a preparation
to prepare. Far too many actors think of
preparation as getting ready to do the scene
or a specific piece of material, and that is
where they start. There is a mandatory step
before this one, however, and that deals
with making your instrument ready to receive
input. This pre-preparation is related to
reaching an authentic BEING state; eliminating
the tension, sensitizing, getting in touch
with everything you feel, and opening the
doors to expression. The exercises in this
chapter will help you only if they are learned, practiced and applied on a daily, living
basis. You can't read a book and learn how
to act, but once you start applying these
exercises you will experience their accumu-
lative results. Each time you repeat an
exercise, using it in all phases of your
life and your work, you will become progressively more skilled at recognizing and alleviating your tension, increasing your awareness and bringing it to the stage. Knowing
the component parts of who you are and using
yourself on and off the stage, and finally,
getting related to other people, is what
life and theatre are all about.

"...getting related to other people is what life and theatre are all about."

III

COMMON SENSORY ACTING

Sense Memory

Throughout my years of teaching, actors have
come to me from all kinds of training; actors who have been Method-trained, actors
who have not been Method-trained, actors
who have brushed with the concept of sense
memory and actors who believed they knew
sense memory well. Some have even been
pompously defensive of their knowledge and
usage of it. My experience has been that
most actors do not understand the concept
of sense memory and do not know how to use
it. They confuse sensory work with pantomime and intellectual gymnastics, neither
of which work in creating realities on
stage. These actors have come from all
the well-established Method teachers in
the country, so obviously sense memory is
either not being communicated clearly, or
it isn't being understood. Because it is
misunderstood and misused, it is maligned
in the business as "Method masturbation."

There are two areas of confusion and misun-
derstanding. First, most people think that
sense memory is an intellectual process and
it is not. It does not take place in the
head. It takes place in the senses. And
second, it's not something you can do once
and expect it to work. Once you truly understand the how of sense memory, you must
practice it daily to make it your own, to
make it work for you. You do it for yourself.

It's your way of creating realities which you personally respond to and which change your life to match the character's life on the stage.

As a teacher I've found that it's essential to be repetitiously specific about how to do the sense memory exercise. And it's equally essential that the actor then take on the responsibility of practicing it daily, weekly, monthly, yearly. Sense memory is one tool in a large tool box. It's not your only tool, but it's an important one. An actor's job is to bring to the stage a human being with a full set of emotions and behavior patterns, a living person who is as unpredictable to himself as he is to the audience who has paid to see him. The circumstances of any drama require the actor to respond to realities which are not real at all. The actress playing his sister is not really his sister. The palace walls are made out of unbleached muslin. He must train his instrument to respond to these imaginary objects as if they really existed by making them real to himself.

We are all a composite of everything that has come in through one or more of our five sensory doors - seeing, hearing, feeling, tasting smelling. Everything we've ever experienced has found its path into our consciousness through our senses and has stimulated some kind of behavior. So it's only common sense to return to your senses to stimulate your behavior on stage. We feel something about everything and everything stimulates some kind of behavior in us. Sense memory is the ability to recreate, through your senses, the object that affected you and impelled you to behave in a certain way.

Before we go into the process of learning to sense memorize an object, we'll give you at

this point a couple of preparatory exercises
for discovering your senses. It's very important for you to find out how your own
senses work, and to be on intimate terms
with your personal instrument, because later,
when you start on sense memory, you'll know
what kinds of questions appeal to your senses. You'll be able to frame the questions
that specifically awaken your senses and
avoid a lot of academic questions that don't
really apply to your apparatus.

1. Sensory Inventory

Read again the description of this exercise
on Page   in Chapter II, and explore it
daily, adding your own discoveries to it
as you go along. Approach it as if it were
an adventure.

2. The Sensory Game

Allot certain times in the day to play this
game and have fun with it. Use all of your
senses and encourage them to relate to all
of the real objects around you, asking yourself all kinds of questions. While you're
eating, for instance, ask yourself how many
different tastes you're aware of and how
many sounds you hear around you. Look at
the room you're in. How many things do you
see? How many different colors can you
find? Notice all of the objects that have
been there a long time which you haven't
paid any attention to. At the same time,
take an emotional inventory and ask yourself
how you feel about each object. You probably won't have a large emotional response
to most objects, but you'll find that you
feel something about everything. Look around
any room for two minutes and then close your
eyes and try to reconstruct the room. Then
open your eyes and try to reconstruct the

room. Then open your eyes and see what you
missed. Run your hand over every object in
a room and ask questions about the different
textures. How is wood different from cloth?
What's the difference between the rug and the
drapes? And how do I feel about those drapes?
Pick up objects which you wouldn't ordinarily
taste and then taste them - a lampshade, a
cigarette box, a flower. The idea is to have
fun and make it exciting.

That picture of your girlfriend or boyfriend -
when was it taken? Do you recall the clothes
you wore that day? Who else was there? Was
it a hot day or rainy and cold? You'll never
run out of questions to ask yourself. You
might suddenly be taken back to another time
and place and reexperenice the same kinds of
feelings you had then. You might find a little
reminiscent smile on your lips. . . well, that's
living. That's an emotional experience which
started by looking at a picture and asking
yourself a few questions.

As you practice the Sensory Game, you'll become much more observant in your daily life
and sensorily alive, as well as increasingly
aware of your personal point of view. At
first, when you do this exercise, your questions will be general, but after a while,
they'll become more complex and you'll be
involved in sensory subtleties. Your questions about how you feel toward these objects
will grow more complex as well. Encourage
yourself to express those feelings. Be quite
deliberate about it. If it's a piece of music
that makes you feel like dancing, then dance!
If it's an odor that offends you, voice your
displeasure. The Game deals only with real
objects, but be assured that after you play
it awhile, your senses will become just as
willing to respond to imaginary objects.

There are no rules except to use all your senses. Make it your own private game and you will find yourself playing it more and more often. Remember the most creative actors are the actors who have the most fun in their work.

JELLYBEAN: NOTHING IS SOMETHING

Application of Sense Memory

The application of sense memory to acting lies in the fact that it trains you to create realities that really don't exist. In a play or a scene, those realities are the place, the character, your relationship to the other person, and the emotional life you must feel according to the circumstances of the material. If you can create a cup of coffee successfully in your hand when it does not exist, create it so that you can taste, smell, feel, see and hear it, then you can create the stimuli that will make you feel those things which the play demands of the character. For example, if your obligation is to be lonely, you can create a place that you have really been lonely in, surrounding yourself with objects that stimulate the feelings of loneliness in you. You can do that here and now, on the stage, so that you are really as lonely as the character in the play. The only difference between the character and the actor is the objects that stimulate the loneliness. You and the character become one. But it all starts with the cup of coffee. If you can't create the coffee, you can't create the place or the loneliness.

3. The Sense Memory Exercise

The importance of the Sense Memory exercise cannot be overstated. It is the cornerstone of the craftual foundation. It's a wise decision to choose to work with something to eat or to drink, because this type of object involves all five of your senses. For practice purposes, always use an object that makes demands on all of the senses, because then you are constantly exercising your total instrument. Later, when you're using sense memory in your choice work, you can isolate one sense for a specific reason. You might want to create a piece of music, using the auditory sense, or work for an odor, which is olfactory. But for now, while you're practicing, it's like practicing scales on the piano and you should practice by exercising all five senses.

After you've selected your object - a glass of milk, a cup of coffee, a piece of candy or fruit - find yourself a place to go to do your work. It should be a comfortable place with a minimum of distractions. It's a good habit to establish a place of work.

Start with any of your five senses. Very soon you'll know which of your senses is the strongest. Use it to encourage the others to respond. Suppose your object is a cup of coffee. From this point forward, get in the habit of referring to any object you work with as "the object" and not as its name. Names and descriptive labels tend to suggest a sensory response rather than evoking it purely in the sense itself. Descriptive words supply your senses with the answer instead of piquing them to respond by themselves. The kinds of answers you want are non-verbal and lie in your fingers, your

ears, your tongue, your eyes - not in language. There is no language in sense memory.
Our senses are conditioned to be lazy through
non-use and they will go to sleep on you unless you appeal to them specifically through
no-name words. Temperature, not hot or cold.
Object, not cup or orange. Size, not inches
or feet. Texture, not rough or smooth. Color,
not red or blue.

Having selected your object, a cup of coffee
with cream and sugar, because cream and sugar
add visual and taste elements (but if you
must have it black, okay), you're ready to
begin the exercise. The order of your physical action will be to place the cup of
coffee on the table, lift the cup to your
mouth, take a swallow and put it back on the
table. Simple as that sounds, it may take you
hundreds of questions and two weeks of daily
practice before you even get the cup to your
mouth. You're about to embark on an amazing
adventure.

Start with the visual sense. The cup is on
the table. Begin by locating it in space
with a spatial question:

- Where is the object on the table?

Respond to that question with your eyes. It
is where you see it is. Then support that
first spatial question with other questions
in the same category:

- How far from the right edge of the table
  does the object sit? Look and see.

- How far is it from the left edge of the
  table?

Again, respond visually. It is as far from

the left edge of the table as your eyes see it
is. Avoid all language-type answers, such as
inches or feet. It is only as far from the
left edge of the table as your eyes tell you
it is.

- What's the distance between the object and
  me?

Let your eyes respond.

- How much of the table area does the object
  cover?

- How wide is the object?

- How high does it stand off the table?

Remember, the only answers are your visual
responses, what your eyes see and tell you.
No words. When asking how high it stands off
the table, you might compare it to another
object on the table. For instance, there
might be a lamp on your table. You could ask:

- How high off the table is the object compared to the lamp? (It's alright to give
  label names to other objects that you're
  not working on.)

This kind of comparative question further sup-
ports the spatial relationship of your object,
because when you begin to work without the
object, these points of comparison help you
to locate it in space.

It's important to note that when you ask a
categorical question (space is a category),
you must support that question with others in
the same category rather than skip to another
category altogether. For instance, if you

ask, "Where is the object?" And then you ask, "What is the color?" - those are two questions from different categories and you've not encouraged your senses to respond to the first question by specifying other questions in that same area of exploration.

There are many other questions you can ask in the spatial category. For example, you might now involve another sense, the tactile, by asking:

- In reaching my hand and arm toward the object, what is the distance that my arm has to travel to make contact with the object?

The purpose of all these questions is to put the object some place in space so that, when you're working without it, you have a definite, specific relationship to where the object was and can recreate it when you're working for the imaginary object.

In any category you can ask twenty, thirty, forty, two thousand questions, depending on your imagination and depending on what the object itself suggests to you, because different objects suggest different questions. It's important for you to realize that the questions are endless. We're giving you seven or eight and you can take it from there. For instance, another spatial question might be:

- If I were to lean back at eye level with the object, how much of the wall behind it does the object obscure?

You can stand up and look down on the object and, in looking down at it, ask:

- From this position, where exactly in relation to the <u>center</u> of the table does the object sit?

Invent your own questions. After you've asked six to ten questions working with the object, put the object aside. Be sure it's entirely out of your view. In trying to recreate the imaginary object, you don't want the real object even in your peripheral view because it will confuse your senses.

Then ask the same group of questions over again and try to respond sensorily to the imaginary object, encouraging yourself to get a sense of it really being there. If other spatial questions that you haven't asked before occur to you now, ask them. Feel free to ask questions that you haven't asked before, if they come to mind, and try to respond visually to those questions. When you've done this, put the real object back in the exact position it was in. Take a quick inventory of where you succeeded in getting responses, where you didn't, and what you may have forgotten.

Now, with the real object in front of you again ask another group of questions. At this point you may want to involve the tactile sense, since you've already asked a visual-tactile question about reaching for the object. Your question might be:

- As I get close to the object with four fingers and thumb, do I begin to anticipate contact anywhere in my hand?

- Do I have any feeling in my fingertips about the anticipated contact?

Answer the questions in those parts of your fingertips where you get even a tingle of response.

134

- How close does my hand come to the object
  before I feel any temperature?

You might feel the bounce of your own body
heat off the object and this is a meaningful
response.

- As I come closer and closer to the object
  with all my fingers, at what point on the
  object and at what point on the finger do
  I first make contact?

This is a triple question, a three-in-one,
involving both visual and tactile. Give
yourself enough time in each sense to respond. Let yourself see the point of contact
on the object. Let yourself see the point
of contact on your finger. And feel the
point of contact on the finger.

- What do I feel in that finger?

The answer to a question about feeling is
the sensation in that part of each finger
and thumb which has made contact with the
object.

- What do I feel as I make contact with the
  other fingers of that hand?

- At how many points on my fingers have I
  made contact?

- Still touching the object lightly, what
  does it feel like?

"Like" means, "What do my fingers interpret
as they feel it?" Don't answer in simile.
Answer with the tactile sense. It feels
like what it feels like. After any group
of questions you may stop and work without
the object, taking inventory of what you
missed or forgot, then continue working

with the real object. Also, if you want, you
may ask the same question over and over again,
working with and without the object, in order
to develop specificity in that one part of a
particular sense.

- What is the texture of the object?

Texture is a supportive question in the category of what it feels like. Texture can also
be its own category.

- What is the difference between what I feel
  texturally in each finger?

Give each finger time to respond individually,
because each finger may, in fact, respond to
that texture differently. There's the possibility that the temperature affects the texture at different points on the object. Your
little finger might be lower down on the objec'
than your middle finger or your index finger
and because the liquid might be at a different
temperature at the lower portion of the object
your little finger might experience moisture,
which would affect the texture.

- Keeping my fingers in one place, do I feel
  a textural difference in any one of them?

- Is there any moisture?

- If so, where?

- How does the sensation of moisture differ
  from the areas of no moisture?

Let your fingers find out all the answers.
Don't say to yourself, "It's dry there, it's
hot there, it's cold there, it's wet there."

- Without moving my fingers, do I feel any
  irregularities?

- If so, how do my fingers know this?

- Can I feel the shape of the object?

Now at this point you might include two or three visual questions:

- What is the overall shape of the object?

- What is the difference between the shape at the top and at the bottom?

- How much wider does it look at the top than at the bottom?

- Where the sides taper, how steep is the angle?

Then piggyback on your visual questions with some tactile ones:

- How does the visual shape differ from what I feel?

- Can I feel the shape?

- Do my fingers feel that taper?

- What is the temperature?

Answer with one finger at a time. Encourage each finger to respond individually. Your questions can weave back and forth between visual and tactile. Suppose there's steam rising from the coffee. You've just experienced the temperature in your fingertips. You might support that with visual clues to the object's temperature:

- Is there steam rising?

- If so, what shapes does it take?

- Can I see any designs in the shapes?

Then return to the tactile exploration:

- What is the temperature?

- How does the temperature vary in each part
  of my hand?

- Do I feel a greater sensation of temperature
  in any part of my fingers?

- If so, where? I just discovered something.
  I just found out I should have asked the
  temperature questions first, because now
  my hand has gotten used to it.

In every Sense Memory exercise you'll make
many discoveries. This is how you'll grow as
a craftsman. You'll find out what kinds of
questions appeal to your senses and to your
emotions. This discovery you made about the
temperature is important and valuable. You
learned that your body adjusts to temperature
very quickly and your first response to temperature is your best. Similarly, in the
olfactory area, your nose will overload quickly, numbing itself to all smells and you'll
have to walk away from the object repeatedly
and return to it fresh. So now, pour yourself a fresh cup of coffee and go on.

- What is the temperature?

- In which finger do I feel it most pronounced?

- Is it different - NOT hotter, warmer, cooler
  - is it DIFFERENT fom my own body temperature?

- What tells me?

- Is the difference uniform or is there a difference in each finger?

138

- With my hand in this position, touching
  the object, has the temperature changed?

- Has my body acclimated to it?

- If so, what does that feel like progressively?

Your hand may have to repeat the action of
contact and withdrawal several times to get
the answer, because once your fingers and
the object have reached the same temperature,
you no longer feel the difference. The time
it takes for your body to acclimate itself
to the object happens rather quickly and in
order to sense memorize that response you
may have to do it as many as a dozen times
before you're able to recreate that interval.

- Are my fingers sweaty?

- Do I feel more moisture between me and the
  object than when I started?

- How does the light affect the object? What
  are the contrasts and highlights?

You're back to the visual sense now.

- Is there a reflection of the light in the
  liquid? Where?

- How does the light affect the texture of
  the receptacle (cup) and the liquid (coffee)?

You may take a sensory trip on this one question of how the light affects the liquid.
Out of this one question may come twenty or
thirty more about the designs and shapes and
hues in the mixture of cream and coffee as
the light affects it. It's fine to take
these trips, because they were sparked by

the object and piqued your interest. But after
awhile it's important to return to the chronology of the exercise.

- How does the light affect the shape of the
  object?

- Are there any distortions? What kind?
  Where?

- Does the light have an affect on the overall
  color of the object? Is the color different
  in the darker portions than it is in the
  lighter parts?

- In looking at the object can I tell where the
  source of light is, where it's coming from?

- Is the object casting a shadow?

- What is the length of the shadow?

- Shape of the shadow? Is there more than one
  shape?

- What pictures do I see in that one shape?

- Does it remind me of anything? Does it suggest anything?

Encourage these kinds of imaginative and inventive questions. The more imaginative and inventive you are, the more fun sense memory
becomes. And if it's fun, you'll practice
more often.
There is no specific number of questions you
should ask before you work without the object.
Ask as many questions at one time as you can
comfortably repeat when working without the
object. However, you might want to ask only
one question, going back and forth between
real and imaginary until you have satisfied

the sensory response. After you have been doing sense memory for a time you will develop your own patterns of exploration. Remember after you've worked with the object, then you work without the object, asking yourself the same sensory questions. Again you go back to the real object to cross check and see what you missed. The entire process is designed so you can ultimately create that cup of coffee, in total, when it is not really there.

Also, while you're practicing your sense memory exercises, it's very important to BE. As you know by now, that means you include everything in your work, all your thoughts and impulses and allow yourself to express them freely. If it's tedium you're experiencing, put that feeling into the questions you ask. Life goes on no matter what you're doing - a scene, a film or a clinical scale playing exercise.

As you do sense memory work, skip around, intermingling your various senses. You could ask three or four visual questions, two or three tactile questions, maybe go back to the visual and pick up where you left off, then ask a couple of olfactory questions, a couple of auditory ones. The sum total might come to twelve or thirteen altogether before you remove the object and work without it. It is encouraged that you intermingle your senses, use them all, but this will always depend on how advanced you are in your sense memory work, how long you've been working with this particular object and whether or not you're purposely isolating a sense and concentrating on it, because it's weak and needs extra work.

On the other hand, for various reasons you may work best if you ask ten or twelve visual

questions, then ten or twelve tactile questions, because perhaps it takes that many
questions to get your senses to start responding. That may be the way you choose to approach the exercise and that's alright. But
ultimately what you want to do is to use your
senses interrelatedly so that one sense picks
up its cue from another. When perceiving an
object sensorily, we often get three responses
at the same time - we see it, hear it and
smell it simultaneously. So this is what you
want to have happen with imaginary objects.
Get into the habit of using the totality of
your sensory apparatus. You can easily create sensory dependencies by leaning too heavil
on one sense and neglecting the others.
Now suppose you're ready to pick up the cup,
to lift it to your mouth and taste the coffee.
You've already investigated it tactually and
your hand is still on the cup. You want to
grasp it so that you can lift it. You might
start with questions like:

- As I apply pressure from my fingers to the
  object, what muscles do I feel tensing?

- What muscles in each finger?

- In my hand?

- In my wrist?

- In my arm?

- Where in my arm?

- How far up my arm do I feel the tension and
  pressure?

Give yourself time to identify the actual sensations in each part of your hand and arm, because when you're working without the object,

the success of recreating it depends on all
those sensations.

- As I squeeze my fingers together, how much
  resistance does the object offer?

- How hard must I squeeze in order to grasp
  the object so that it won't slip through
  my fingers?

- How does the resistance of the object affect the tension in my fingers?

- As I press into the object, how does the
  object penetrate into my fingerpads?
  Visual and tactile - I see it and I feel
  it.

- How much of each finger is obscured by the
  object in relation to the angle I'm sitting
  in?

As you were working for the pressure of the
object on your fingers, it became obvious
to you that there were fingers you couldn't
see. So this last question presented itself
and you dealt with it. Always respect the
chronology of sensory elements that occur
while you're working and answer them. To
ignore these questions when they come up
would violate the natural reality.

- Into which finger do I feel the most pene-
  tration? What does that feel like?

- Can I feel bone contact? What does that
  feel like?

Any of these questions may demand twenty
other questions to capture all the subtleties of that one question. You'll find
this out when you're working without the
object. You'll find out how much more

specific and how many questions you need in
that particular area to get a sense of the
object.

- Now I feel ready to lift the object. What
  must I do to lift the object? What is my
  first movement? Where does it start?

- Does it start in the arm or in the hand?

- Where in the arm do I begin to lift upward?
  What does that feel like?

- As I do that, what is the first movement I
  see taking place in the object?

- What sounds do I hear related to the object?

- Can I hear the liquid sloshing?

- What are the component parts of that subtle
  sound?

- With which ear do I perceive that?

- What other sounds do I hear in the room?

- What is the predominant sound? Where is it
  coming from?

- As I slowly move my arm upward, how does it
  affect the liquid?

- As I move my hand slowly upward to lift the
  object, how does it tilt?

- What part of the object leaves the table first?

- Can I hear that?

- What muscles am I now using that I wasn't using
  before? Where do I feel them? What does it
  feel like?

- When do I begin to feel the increased weight now that the object is off the table?

- What is weight? What is it? What do I mean by weight in terms of what I'm feeling?

- How do I feel weight? Where in my fingers, hand, wrist and arm do I feel that thing that I call weight?

- What is the downward pressure that the object exerts on my fingers, my hand, my wrist?

- How far up the arm do I feel that pull?

- As I move the object toward my face, how does the weight change?

- What other muscles come into play?

- What other pressures do I feel?

- What about the fatigue factor? I've been holding it here a long time. Where are my muscles beginning to get tired and how does that feel? What are the sensations of fatigue?

- As I move it close to my face, how much more of the liquid can I see?

- And in this new position how far down into the object can I see?

- Is the liquid moving as a result of the movement of my hand?

- Where in my hand do I feel the movement of that liquid?

145

- As I move the cup around in small circles,
  where in my hand do I feel the sloshing of
  the liquid?

- Can I hear that?

- What other weight changes take place as I
  move closer to my face?

- As I get closer, at what point do I begin
  to feel the temperature? Where on my face
  do I feel that temperature?

- Is there steam? Where do I feel it? Where
  does it emanate? What does it look like?

- What is the difference between the temperature of the liquid as I get it close to my
  face and the temperature of my face around
  the area that's not being affected? Can I
  distinguish a difference?

- At what point do I begin to smell the object

- What is smell? Where do I smell? What do I
  mean by smell?

- Where in my nose, in my nostrils, do I smell

- How many different odors do I detect?

- What are those differences?

- Can I smell the cream? The sugar? The coffee? The object itself?

- As I bring it closer, do I smell more?

- How many other odors am I aware of around me

- With which nostril do I smell the most? I
  might have to block each nostril with my
  other hand to answer that question.

At any point you may want to stop and work
with and without the object in small areas.
For instance, when the object is closest to
your face, you're seeing, smelling, feeling,
hearing all at once. Your senses are being
flooded with stimulation. So you might have
to break it down and take it in small hunks,
working separately with each sense and then
putting it together.

- In lifting the object to my mouth to taste
  it, what is the angle of my hand? The
  angle of my arm? Where is my arm in relation to my shoulder? In relation to my
  head? Where? How high? What do I see?

- How high is my hand in relation to the
  height of the table?

- As I approach my mouth and begin tilting
  my head to receive the liquid, how far
  back do I tilt my head?

- What angle is my head in relation to the
  table?

- What do I see as my head goes back?

- As my head goes back, at what point on the
  ceiling do my eyes stop? What is that
  visual point?

- As I bring the object up to my lips, how
  intense does the temperature get on my
  lips? Where do I feel that?

- What do I see at this point, with the object
  so close? Is it blurred?

- What part of the cup touches my lip first?

- Which lip first? Bottom or top?

- As it touches my lip, how does it feel specifically at the contact point? How does it feel radiating outward from that point?

- Temperature? Texture? What part of the lip feels the most?

- How long does it take for the lip to get accustomed to the temperature of the object?

- As my top lip touches the object, how much difference between the top lip and the bottom What do I feel with the top lip?

- As the liquid goes into my mouth, what part of my mouth does it hit first?

- Exactly at that moment of contact of the liquid in my mouth, what do I feel?

- What is the temperature? What is the sensation of temperature?

- What is the difference in temperature between the inside of my mouth and the liquid? What in my mouth tells me that?

- What is temperature, what is heat in terms of the feeling I'm getting in my mouth?

- What is the path of the liquid as it runs into my mouth? What parts of my mouth does it run into?

- What are the many different sensations I'm experiencing in my mouth?

- Can I smell it internally?

- As the liquid runs back into my mouth, are there any sensitive teeth? Do I feel any pain in any parts of the gums and inner cheek?

- How long does it take for the liquid to equalize to my mouth's temperature?

- What is the consistency of the liquid? What does it feel like on my tongue - what parts of my tongue?

- What are the taste sensations? Where do I begin to taste?

- What is taste?

- Where in my mouth am I actually tasting what I taste?

- How many different tastes can I identify?

- Can I distinguish the separate ingredients of the liquid? Where? What do they taste like?

- Can I taste the difference between the coffee and the cream? Can I taste the sugar? Where do I taste sugar? (Specifically, break it down)

- What happens in my mouth as I begin to swallow? The various muscular activities? What does my tongue do? What does the head do?

- Where does the swallow begin?

- As I open my throat to receive the liquid, what muscles come into play?

- What do I feel when the liquid begins to run down into my throat?

Once you've done the exercise to the swallowing of the liquid, you must replace the cup on the table. This is still part of the exercise, because it is essential to keep

149

the reality going to its logical conclusion.
The cup cannot vanish in thin air. As you
go through this final section of the exercise, continue asking sensory questions in
the order in which they present themselves
down to the final auditory sounds of the
cup hitting the table.

When you have spent many hours working with
and without the object and breaking it down
into small areas of exploration, then you
should do the entire exercise straight
through without referring back to the real
object. Recreate it totally from your sensory memory. Not only is this the logical
progression of sense memory but, when working in a play or a film, you must be able to
create your choice, totally, without the
presence of the real object.

The beauty of sense memory is that you have
very few limitations. You can practice it
anywhere, at any time and it takes no special equipment. You can work for heat in a
chilly room. You can make music in deadly
silence. You can create beautiful things on
ugliness. The world is at the command of
your imagination through the magic of your
five doors of perception.

JELLYBEAN: SENSE MEMORY WON'T WORK FOR YOU
             UNLESS YOU WORK FOR IT.

About The Sense Memory Exercise

Two of the most important purposes of sense
memory are your instrumental development -
the training of your senses to be alive and
responsive - and the development of your
ability to create whatever realities you
need to make you feel what the character

150

feels. Sense memory will not pay off, however, unless you practice it daily over a
period of time and make it a part of your
life. If you really commit yourself to it
you will find it to be a backbone tool for
you which ultimately will elicit unconscious
organic responses of astounding dimension.

Ask as many questions as you need in order
to recreate the object. As you go along,
you'll find your own rhythm, your own sensory needs. In the beginning, your instrument may require more questions than later
on. In certain sensory areas you may have
to ask many more questions than other areas,
if that's a weaker sense for you. You might
have to isolate one question and ask thirty
related to it before the sense responds to
that specific thing. Also, the nature of
the object will often dictate its own investigation.

Choosing objects is a very important area.
What is an object? For our purposes, an object can be anything, animate or inanimate,
not just something you can see and pick up.
An object can also be a sound, a smell, a
temperature, a person, an animal, a time of
year. At first, as we've said earlier, choose
objects to eat or drink because they engage
all five senses. As you progress, you'll
find many reasons behind your choice of an
object. To improve a sluggish tactile sense,
you might spread fifty different objects out
on a table, all with a variety of textures,
and close your eyes and investigate them all
tactilly. If your auditory sense needs work,
you might blindfold yourself and navigate
around the room just on the basis of sounds,
or you might work with one object which is
primarily sound-producing - a bell, a piece
of music.

Choose objects which excite you, which interest you emotionally and sensorily, so that
you don't get bored. Also choose objects
with an awareness of their potential challenge to your senses. An object without any
patterns or colors, something that has a
bland, standard kind of shape doesn't really
give your senses much of an adventure. Pick
things with an eye to their complexity.

After you've been working with sense memory
for awhile, you'll choose objects quite individually to deal with your own sensory problems and you may be in the process of working
with three or four different kinds of objects
at the same time, each for different reasons.
Sometimes you'll select something to work on
just for clinical purposes to exercise your
senses, as a pianist would stretch his fingers. You'll want to make yourself remain
on that academic level to discipline your
senses as an antidote to sloppiness. When
you've been doing sense memory a long time,
you tend to lapse into generalities and take
things for granted. A purely academic workout gets you back on the track. But even
though you start clinically, your exercises
should all be adventures. Sense memory is
something you should look forward to, anti-
cipating it as a game you love to play, a
sojourn into the unknown.

Following is a list of questions, a kind of
checklist to help you understand and apply
the sense memory exercise. Don't use it like
a pilot's checklist, literally checking out
each item each time you take off. It's an
overall map of elements, which eventually you
will assimilate. Look it over before you
begin and then put it aside. Soon the checklist will be internalized and become part of
your work.

Sense Memory Check List

- Am I asking enough questions?

- Am I asking the questions specifically?
  Do my senses understand the questions?

- Am I asking the right kinds of questions?
  Not intellectual ones, but the ones that
  appeal to my senses?

- Do my questions interest me? Do they affect me emotionally?

- Am I really concentrating on the object or
  am I just concentrating on concentrating?

- How do I feel? (Personal Inventory)

- Are my questions coming in logical sequence
  or are they violating the chronological
  order?

- Am I asking inventive, imaginative questions?

- Am I using my time well, allowing enough
  time to encourage my senses to answer, giving them enough time to respond?

- Do I have any tension? If so, where is it?
  Am I including it? And how can I alleviate
  it?

- Am I doing it for me?

- Am I getting a sense of the object? Do I
  really feel it, smell it, taste it or am I
  kidding myself?

- Am I being too precious or teensy-weensy?
  Am I being pedantic and specifying what is
  already specific?

- Am I unpredictable? Am I surprising myself?

- Am I tricking myself now and then?

- What does the object remind me of or suggest to me?

- Am I including everything that's going on, my thoughts, my feelings and distractions, and am I expressing these with the exercise?

- Am I letting the object suggest its own exploration?

- How can I have more fun and make it more of an adventure?

- Am I letting the exercise kick off thoughts and impulses that take me on a trip and am I allowing myself to go with that, without letting these digressions become endless?

- Am I really working sensorily or just suggestively?

- Do I allow myself to start with any sense or am I dependent on the same one?

- Have I located the object in space?

- Am I asking supportive questions in each category?

- Am I using the stronger senses to encourage the weaker ones?

- Am I asking hundreds, thousands of questions?

- Am I finding my sensory triggers?

- Do I let myself walk away for awhile when it becomes too tedious?

Marathon: Sense Memory Round

The scene: A Marathon, January 12, 1972.
A marathon acting session occurs every few
months and is attended by a group of fifteen
or twenty of my students who want to work at
their craft intensively for twenty-four hours
straight. At the moment, the group is sitting in a circle doing an exercise called
The Sense Memory Round. Each actor is working with his own inanimate object. One at
a time, each actor asks a group of sensory
questions out loud about his object and the
other actors in the Round respond sensorily
to those questions in relation to their own
objects. After five or ten questions, I call
on the next person to continue, but I don't
go "around the circle" in order, because I've
found that actors build up tension knowing
when their turn is coming. The next person
picks up where the last one left off and goes
on in any direction from there.

Corinne: (Working with a small china statue)
Where is it light and where is it
dark on the object?

Eric : Not a good question to start that
category, because you're drawing a
conclusion by calling it light and
dark instead of making your senses
work.

Corinne: How does the light affect the object?

Eric : Better. Much better.

Corinne: Which part of the object is exposed
directly to the light?

155

Eric   : Good. That kind of question encourages your visual sense to investigat
rather than accept a conclusion.
Okay, Norman?

Norman: (Working with a paperweight) I'm
experiencing the weight.

Eric   : No. Ask a question about the weight

Norman: (A silence) I'm asking myself the
question.

Eric   : Ask it out loud.

Norman: What is weight? What does it feel
like when it touches my palm? Ex-
tending from the back of my hand.

Eric   : That's a whole book you've asked.
I don't understand the question.
It's too fast, it's too widespread
a question. It's not specific
enough. Too general. Do you know
what I mean by too general?

Norman: No, I don't know what that means.

Eric   : Alright, here's a specific question
about the weight. 'How does the
weight of the object affect my hand
in terms of the downward pressure I
feel? Exactly where in my hand do
I feel that downward pressure?'
Norman, don't shake the object back
and forth. Just keep it still in
your hand and ask a question.

Norman: How does it feel in my palm? Where
are the points of. . .

Eric   : Before you pile on another question,
give your palm a chance to respond.

Norman: (After a pause) Where are the points of contact?

Eric : Good.

Norman: Where is it hard and soft?

Eric : No, no, hard and soft are answers. They're conclusions. The texture, the resiliency, the mass, the resistance of the object - those are the areas you ask questions in. If you use a word like texture, then your senses must supply the answers. Now slow it down, Norman. Go on.

Norman: Where is the air space between the points of contact?

Eric : Good. Very good. That's much more specific. Do you feel any responses to that? (Norman nods yes.) Cindy?

Cindy : (Working with an orange) How does the object feel on my fingers?

Eric : Finger first, then fingers. You're doing too much too fast, Cindy.

Cindy : Where do I feel the object on each finger?

Eric : Good. Take the time to answer with each finger.

Cindy : What are the differences in what each finger feels?

Eric : Good. I'd like you to pursue that. Leave the round awhile and work over in that corner. Guy?

157

Guy :   What is the temperature? (Pause) Whe
        do I feel it? (Pause? What is the di
        ference between the temperature of the
        object and the temperature of my hand?

Eric: Good questions. Good usage of time,
        Guy. John?

John: (He's working with an ashtray full of
        cigarette butts and an orange peel. H
        asks three or four questions in the
        area of temperature, picking up where
        Guy left off, and then goes to the ol-
        factory sense.) What do I smell?
        (Pause) How many odors am I aware of
        around me? (Pause) What's the strong
        est smell? (Pause) Can I smell the
        object from here? (The ashtray is on
        the rug about three feet below him.)
        As I bring my head toward the object,
        when does the odor increase? (Pause)
        As I lift the object, how close. . .

Eric: Wait a minute, John. You were doing
        great until then, but now you're vio-
        lating the logical order of the re-
        ality. Something has to take place
        before you lift the object. Right?

John: Oh, yeah, Eric. I was just concen-
        trating on the olfactory.

Eric: Do it chronologically, John, because
        I don't want you to violate everyone
        else's reality.

John: Okay. How much pressure must I apply
        in my fingers so that I can grasp the
        object?
Eric: Good.
John: Where is the muscular tension in each

Group of actors doing Sense Memory round at a marathon.

finger? (John is an experienced
student and gives himself enough
time between each question.) In
the hand? Wrist? Up the arm? How
far up the arm before I feel any
muscular tension? What does the
resistance from the object feel
like?

Eric   : Pamela, why are you crying?

Pamela: I'm working for my dog. I loved
him and he's dead.

Eric   : Pam, I don't want you to work for
your dog. Everybody's working on
inanimate objects today for a purpose. Inanimate objects are much
easier to work with because they're
constant, they stay the same. Animate objects are always changing,
moving, blinking, breathing, going
away, coming back, and all these
things must be dealt with when
you're working with animate objects.
To work on a living thing - a person, an animal, you must have a
greater degree of sensory sophisti-
cation and facility. That's not to
say I discourage any of you from
working on a person or an animal at
any stage of your training, but be
aware that you cannot approach it
as an unchanging object. For today,
in this Sensory Round, I want us to
stick with inanimate objects.

Pamela: Eric, I'm really _feeling_ something
right now! Why are you stopping me?

Eric   : I've no desire to stop you from
feeling what you're feeling. But
tell me, how did you get to that?

Pamela: (Angry and sobbing) Well, I remembered this dog I used to have and I pictured her lying in front of me with blood all over her and I remembered how I felt when she was run over.

Eric : Pam, I don't disbelieve your feelings, but as your teacher I feel responsible for your process. Your process was intellectual and suggestive and the emotional response from that kind of work is not dependable because it's retrospective.

Pamela: What do you mean, Eric? It worked for me.

Eric : Yes, but would it work for eight performances a week? Or will it evaporate on you because it isn't coming from a solid reality? Now, Pam, don't get me wrong. I don't mean for a moment that if something works for you , if something stimulates in you an organic, three-dimensional response and does it consistently - even if you say one word to yourself and it happens to you everytime - I don't argue with that. And I'm saying this to all of you. Whatever works for you WORKS. Go with that, if it works consistently. You don't have to go through the sensory process, you don't have to go through any process, if you've got something that is truly real for you. Talent is talent. I never negate talent.

But Pam, what I saw you do, the reason I stopped you - now this is really important for you to understand -

what I saw was something I call theatrical hysteria. You were crying
and sobbing and lying on the carpet
and talking about your dog, but it
was coming out of tension and anxiety
and your obligation to succeed and
impress. I don't mean show off, but
to be good as an actress. We all
want to be good. That passes for
real emotion on television and in
the theatre and you're very good at
that, Pam, but I stopped you because
I don't want you to settle for that.
It's conventional. It's shallow and
predictable. I want you to be able
to achieve a depth of meaning, an
organic reality, a three-dimensional,
unpredictable reality that comes out
of a real choice. I believe you're
capable of doing that. For now you
are going to have to let go of something that you can do to reach for
something that you can't yet do, but
something that will be infinitely
more exciting for your work. I understand how terrifying it is to let
go and seemingly have nothing for a
while, but Pam, I'm urging you to do
it, because the rewards will be phenomenal.

Pamela: What rewards, Eric? I'm so confused.
I don't know where to go. I don't
understand what any of this has to
do with my dog.

Eric : Okay, listen. I had a dog. The
dog's name was Holly. The dog was
about so big and kind of tan, whatever. Okay. Holly died. I feel
sad that Holly died. However, before
she died a lot of years passed. There
were a lot of feelings I had about

163

Holly and if I want to recreate that
relationship and feel those things I
felt toward the dog and even some of
the unconscious things I felt toward
her, I must be capable of creating
that animal here in front of me as
that animal existed when it was a-
live. You follow me so far?

Pamela: I think so.

Eric : Okay. Now, in order to do that I
must have a process of sensory memory so that I can create that animal
in total, not just when she died
with blood all over her, but hear
her, feel her, see her and if I
wanted to, taste her. Now this is
not an intellectual process. I do
not think about how Holly was when
she sat there. I do not picture
her, because that's just suggesting
that the whole object is there instantly, without creating the component parts, which will make it
fully real to me. I do not remember
the sounds and smells in my head, because my brain does not have a nose.
It doesn't have ears. My nose is my
nose, my ears are my ears and those
are the places I smell and hear. If
all I do is remember how I felt about
Holly, the memory of that feeling
will not restimulate that feeling at
all, only an intellectual, retrospective shadow of that feeling. I can
remember that I felt sad and in doing
so I might again feel sad about being
sad.

However, if I want to have a three-
dimensional relationship to my dog,

164

here and, now even to my dog being
dead, I must first create my dog so
that I can really relate to her. I
must create her so that I can see
her, smell her, hear her, feel her,
taste her. I might even laugh. I
might play with the dog. I might
tickle the dog. The dog might bite
my arm. The dog might run away from
me. The dog must exist for me here
and now. If the dog exists and I'm
responding to it in terms of its
reality, I can then work for the
dog being dead. At that point I
will respond to the dog's death totally, very dimensionally, honestly
---as if it were happening here and
now, because in fact it is.

Now to be able to do that, I have to
know, one, how my senses function
and, two, how to make them aware and
receptive and, three, the technical
process of making them do my bidding
and work for me and, four, I have to
practice them. If I tell you how to
do this tonight, you cannot come
back tomorrow night and create your
dog. Not tomorrow. Maybe after a
lot of tomorrows. We're at the very
first step in the creative process
here and I'm going to forget about
Holly for now because Holly is a
very complicated living object that
constantly changes. What I'm doing
now with this inanimate object, this
apple, this pencil, is I'm training
my senses to sense memorize it with
the purpose of recreating this object's existence when it does not
exist anymore. In doing so, I can
later create Holly and my mother and

is a special place for me. Over the
years it's become not only my sleep
place, but also my office, my play-
ground and my rehearsal hall. In fact,
in a Pavlovian way my bed actually
stimulates me to work (which sometimes
messes up my sleeping schedule!) When
I want to find a choice or try out a
choice to see where it takes me, the
first thing I do is get on my bed.
It's my magic place.

Early morning is often a good time for
me to work, because I'm just rested
enough, but still tired enough not to
care too much. I have a tendency to
try too hard and push for results, but
at two-thirty in the morning I'm grate-
ful if I feel anything at all. My mind
is still foggy, so I don't get over-
complex. My sensory responses happen
naturally and simply and that pleases
me and makes me want to do more. Also
at that time of the day I feel particularly vulnerable and alone, hanging
out in space while everyone else is
sleeping. For that reason I use this
time to work on meaningful choices too,
besides the bedside objects, because my
defenses are down, my skin is thinner,
and everything affects me more quickly
and deeply.

Sensory Exploration and Experimentation

The following group of exercises deal with
your development in the sensory world. All
of them relate in one way or another to discovery, exploration, and experimentation with
your self and the objects in the world around

you. If sense memory becomes an adventure
that you look forward to, then you will begin to experience the magic of this work and
eventually take possession of a powerful
tool in the creative process.

4. Sense Memory Looked Forward To

Sense Memory Looked Forward To is a device,
a way of getting yourself to enjoy and therefore practice sense memory. There are many
things people enjoy and look forward to
doing - having your back massaged, sitting
in a hot tub after a long day's work, sensual
pleasures, listening to your favorite piece
of music, a glass of good wine. Whatever you
look forward to doing in real life can make
an excellent sense memory exercise and if you
enjoy it, you'll be more likely to practice
sense memory.

5. Feelies

A feelie is any object you can carry in your
pocket or purse. A feelie is also a smellie,
a tastie, a hearie and a seeie. I used to
carry all kinds of feelies in my pockets.
My pockets looked like a junk shop - little
bottles of liquid sen-sen, pieces of fabric,
small stones, a rabbit's foot, a perfumed
sachet. Waiting around in offices, I'd take
something out of my pocket and work on it.
Sitting in a restaurant having coffee and
watching the world go by I'd take three or
four objects out and lay them on the table
and alternate between them.

6. Sense Memory Workout

- Get familiar with an inanimate object.

- Work without it.

my father and my uncle and all those
people and objects that affected me
deeply.

JELLYBEAN:
IF BOTH HANDS ARE FULL OF FOOL'S GOLD,
HOW CAN YOU PICK UP THE REAL GOLD?

*Sense memory should become a part of your way
of life.* Daily sit-down practice is only one
aspect of it, although an important one, because you could practice it every day and even
be quite facile in it, but not have it be a
part of your life. Sense memory must belong
to your philosophy. It's an integral part of
your craft and your craft is more than a way
of working. It's a way of living. Sensory
work must profoundly influence the way you
relate to things and perceive them. It's a
continual process of looking and feeling and
assimilating, breaking up the sensory component parts of objects that you can use later,
and making on-the-spot discoveries of things
that affect you. It should be happening with
you always - riding on a bus, in a car, on a
date with your lover, eating dinner, at a
party. Wherever you are and whatever you're
going through, you are constantly identifying
the sensory elements and understanding how
they affect you so that you can recreate
those things right now or tomorrow or next
month. You are cataloguing your life's experiences for future use on stage and you are
also opening your instrument, each day expanding yourself to be more available to many
more things.
Even though the process begins consciously at
a point where you have to remind yourself to
ask questions about what's going on around
you, ultimately it becomes automatic. You
take a mountain walk and hardly realize that

you're listening for different sounds and collecting the various outdoor odors. Actors often complain, "I can't remember anything below the age of ten and even the stuff I remember, I can't recall how they smelled or tasted." Starting from today forward, take inventories of yesterday and the day before and this habit will gradually open up your sensory memory of earlier times in your life, building your repertoire of choices. Your conscious exploration releases your unconscious reservoir, and all kinds of colors from your unconscious begin flowing into your work. *The unconscious is where your real talent lives.*

Your sensory quest should go on twenty-four hours a day (dreaming is sensory too!), every day of your life.

Finding Your Best Time and Place to Work

You should do at least forty-five minutes to an hour of sit-down daily practice on inanimate objects. Choose the best time for you, the time when you are least distracted, most comfortable and most excited about sensory exploration. The place can be anywhere. Find a place you enjoy.

Joan: I'm a day person and I like to go to bed early. But often I wake up early in the morning, two-thirty, five o'clock, with a vague sense of unfinished business, which I relieve with an hour or two of sensory work and then I go back to sleep again. I keep by my bedside a few of my current objects - a hollow-stemmed champagne glass, a stone, a small pinecone, perfume, cough drops, etc. My king-sized bed

- Get familiar with an animate object, person, animal.

- Work without it.

- Get familiar with some physical part of your own self.

- Work without it.

- Get familiar with an external object or body contact; hat, cape.

- Work without it.

- Get familiar with a sound or smell.

- Work without it.

7. What-Not Boxes

This is an exercise for blind sensory investigation. A little what-not box is something you can construct. It's about two feet by two feet, all sides enclosed except for a hole in one side just big enough to get your hand in. Have someone in your family or a friend fill it with small objects that appeal to all the senses, a wide variety of them. Then, without knowing what's in there, put your hand in and, just by feeling each object, try to decide what it looks like, what its true shape is, what color it might be, what it might smell like, what sound it would make if it dropped to the floor. Supply these imaginary answers sensorily just by the tactile clues. Then take the objects out of the box and really find out how they look, taste, sound, and smell.

A big what-not box is your house or a room in it. With your eyes closed move around the room smelling, tasting, hearing and feeling

everything. Sensorily identify and explore
the objects that you are visually familiar
with and be aware of your sensory responses
to objects that your sight has taken for
granted. When you look at a fabric, your
bedspread or draperies, you really don't
know how it feels or tastes or smells. But
when you're blind and you feel it, it takes
on a whole new life. You'll find all tastes
and smells and sounds become more vivid.

8. On-The-Spot Sense Memorizing

Every day you will experience many things.
Pick a fleeting experience - a bus passes
you and the fumes hit you in the face - a
telephone ringing in another room - your
first sip of cold beer on a hot day at the
beach - and just after it's gone, try to
recreate the sensations in a minute or two.
Keep it simple. Don't try to recreate too
much. Ask maybe ten to twenty questions.
You can do this fifty times a day with fifty
different things. This exercise allows you
to work for the imaginary elements shortly
after you experience the real elements. As
you do it over a period of time you collect
more and more objects to be used in the
future. And it disobligates you from having
to do a complete sense memory exercise every
time you decide to practice.

9. Kinesthetics

The kinesthetic sense, described in Chapter
II, is your muscular response to the presence
or absence of objects around you. With your
eyes closed, walk around slowly and care-
fully and try to sense the objects and people
around you without touching anything. Use
your kinesthetic sense to determine distances
and positions of objects. It's fun to do it
in the park in a large, open space with

another actor who (with his eyes open) moves in and out of your kinesthetic range. After a while you really begin to know where he is.

10. Sense Memory Guessing Games

These games include all the senses. They're good to play with friends, with actors at rehearsals, at parties, but you can also do them alone. One version is a group sitting in a room with their eyes closed and one person walks around tapping things, dropping things, making sounds of all kinds, holding odiferous objects under people's noses for identification. Identification is the way you win and when you think you have an answer you raise your hand and say where the sound comes from and what materials are involved in making that sound - metal, plastic, wood. The leader can pass around a tray with three or four jars of different substances, such as honey, cottage cheese, ketchup, sour cream. Each person sticks one finger in and without smelling it or tasting it, describes out loud the sensation. The results of this one are often hilarious. The solo version of the exercise is also entertaining. Sitting in your house and listening to the cars go by, try to identify the makes by their sounds. Open the kitchen cupboard, close your eyes, and use your sense of smell and touch to know whatever is in there. Invent your own versions of these games.

11. Get A Sense Of Being Naked

Do this exercise fully clothed. Of course, to achieve success in it you will have had to practice it with and without clothes, as you do in all sense memorizing. It's delicious to do this exercise secretly while at a party or a wedding, because it produces a startling effect on your behavior. If you're

really successful in creating a sense of
your own nudity, you'll experience all kinds
of unpredictable things. When people look
down at you, you'll get embarrassed and turn
away. You'll find yourself blushing or gig-
gling or behaving in sensually provocative
ways. It engages the overall use of your
body and you should use your whole body frequently to remind yourself that sense memory
is not just your hand on a cup or your nose
to a lemon. These fun-producing exercises
will encourage you to do sense memory all
the time.

12. Recreate A Moment From Today

Pick a moment of today when something vivid
happened. It doesn't have to be a strong
emotional event. It can be something pleasant and warm - you had lunch with a friend,
you bought something you liked. Isolate a
sensory element of the experience and try to
recreate it. You had lunch today with a
friend you hadn't seen in a long time. You
were in an open patio restaurant and you
really enjoyed the nostalgic dialogue of
things you shared in the past. Out of the
complexity of this experience you might
choose to work for one sensory element of
the warm afternoon sun on your face while
you and your friend were talking. Recreate
how that felt on your face specifically,
the direction of the sun, the degree of
heat, the difference in what you felt in
each part of your face, etc. By doing just
that, there's a strong possibility that you
might re-experience some of the feelings
you had that afternoon. And maybe you won't.
Working for that element is enough.

13. Animate An Inanimate Object

This is more of a game than it is a sense

memory exercise, but it involves the senses
and it's fun. It also stimulates your imagination. Take an inanimate object - a chair,
a pencil, a typewriter - and endow it with a
personality as sensorily as possible. Try to
create its voice and really hear it. Give it
movement, rhythm, visual activities such as
crossing the room. Have an imaginary conversation with the object. Do it with all kinds
of objects, anywhere and at any time.

14. The Desert Exercise

This is a marvelous sense memory exercise.
When done with a group of people, it can also
be an improvisation. You're stranded in the
desert and the point is to create all the
elements of exposure, exhaustion, thirst,
heat, the vastness of your isolation. Begin
with one element - for instance, the heat.
Start by making the room you're in hotter
than it is. Then you might go to creating
the desert around you visually, locating
where the sun is. These elements support
your working for heat. It may take you two
weeks of doing the exercise to work up a
sweat. Then go on, progressively adding
one element at a time of the total reality.
If you're successful, the heat itself may
stimulate thirst. It's an excellent sensory
workout and the rewards are very satisfying.
The Desert Exercise is not recommended for
people who are just beginning to do the work
of sense memory.

Working With Meaningful Objects

In the application of sense memory to acting,
your first step is to go from clinical practice with inanimate objects to objects which
are meaningful to you. A meaningful object

is anything that evokes an emotional response
in you no matter how slight. In your sensory
exploration you've undoubtedly come upon objects that have some kind of emotional impact
on you. Now work on these meaningful objects
deliberately, besides your apples and oranges,
and form the habit of affecting yourself emotionally through the sense memory process.
At this point you are not concerned with the
emotional needs of a piece of dramatic material. Don't burden yourself yet with this
obligation. As you become skilled at affecting yourself emotionally through sense memory,
you should begin then to deal with dramatic
material. After working with many meaningful
objects you will know what kinds of things
sound good, but don't affect you, as compared
to the objects that really touch you.

Here are some suggestions of meaningful objects. Hopefully they will stimulate other
ideas.

- Photographs

- Childhood toys

- A family pet

- Highschool yearbook

- Love letters

- Pressed flowers

- Your children

- Theatrical reviews

- A piece of jewelry

- Any of your bedrooms as you grew up

- A piece of meaningful music

- Any meaningful place in your life
  (Army barracks, Kindergarten, Summer Camp)

- Your mother

- Your father

- Your wife, husband, lover

Obligation and Choice

It is necessary now to define obligation and
choice and how they relate to sense memory.

An obligation is that which exists in the
scene that indicates to you what the character
feels. That becomes what you want to feel.
For instance, the character in the scene feels
despondent, alone, without goal direction,
suicidal. Those are your obligations in the
scene. Those are all the things that you
want to feel.

A choice is the object you choose to make you
feel what the character feels. *Sense memory
is the way you create the choice.* Your choice
is the stimulus you will use sensorily to create the kind of behavior and emotional life
you want in the scene. Your choice might be
to recreate a simple piece of music, a certain
melody that makes you feel despondent and a-
lone. A choice can be almost anything. A
place, a time and a place, a piece of furniture, a person, an aroma, a sound, the kinesthetic feeling of the presence of someone
outside the door or in back of you, a piece
of clothing, an external sense of being something other than what you are, such as an

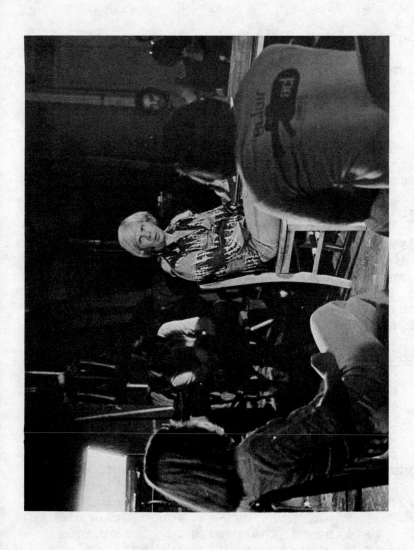

Eric teaching a film directing course at U.S.C. — the same work,

177

object or an animal or another person. A
choice can be anything that works for you.
You choose it in the hopes of stimulating
not only a single identifiable emotion, but
also a complicated emotional life.

Some choices need not be translated sensorily,
because the approach to creating the object
is clear. You're working for a certain of-
fensive odor, because your obligation is to
feel nauseous. It's a clear sense memory
exercise. Or you're working for an award
you won, a gold statuette, because it makes
you feel accomplished and proud. These are
both simple objects and all you do to create
them is ask the questions and answer them
with your senses.

But some choices require sensory translation
before you can begin the process of creating
them. For instance, if you want to restimulate the hurt you felt when a certain person
criticized you over the telephone, where
would you begin? Ask yourself what exactly
was it that made you feel hurt. Your answer
will be what that person said to you over the
phone. Since you cannot create that voice
out of mid-air, you start by sensorily creating the telephone in your hand and at your
ear. Then once you have a sense of the telephone, you create the voice, the sound of it,
the pitch, the rhythm, the peculiarities of
it. Finally you create the words themselves
which hurt you. You will know when you have
to translate a choice sensorily, simply because reality dictates its own order. If
your starting point on a choice is obvious
to you, then start. If you don't know where
to start, you will have to translate that
choice sensorily before creating it. The
translation is just a device which tells you
where to start and how to work for your choice.

The trip from your practice training with
coffee cups and inanimate objects to the ful-
filling of a strong emotional obligation,
such as a character about to commit suicide,
is a long trip. It begins with your first
sit-down sensory exercise. Your ability to
create a cup of coffee so that you can really
see it, feel it, taste it, smell it, hear it,
is the same ability that you must have to
create the objects necessary to make you feel
suicidal. That's the connection between coffee cups and suicide.

Using Sense Memory in Scene Work

Before finishing this chapter, we want to give
you an example of how obligation, choice and
the sensory approach fit together in a scene.
The following is a taped excerpt from a class
demonstration. For the last several weeks,
Lori and Allen have been working on a scene
adapted from Hemingway's short story, "The
Hills Are Like White Elephants". I'm using
the circumstances of this material to illus-
trate some points to the class. . .

(The Tape)

Eric: If I were doing a scene with Lori and
we were lovers and we'd been living
together for a long time and she's
pregnant and I feel guilty about it
and yet I love her and I don't want
her to have the baby - those are the
realities and obligations in the material. Okay, the first thing I must
feel is love for her, because unless
I care about her I can't feel guilty
or have any of those conflicts. So
I'll start simply with the obligation
to love her. And before deciding on

what to work for, I'll start with what
exists.

How do I feel about Lori? I feel warm
and affectionate about her. I like
her. But that isn't enough to fulfill
the obligation. So I need a choice.
Instead of creating things in Lori I
love, knowing me and my needs, it would
be easier to love someone if I could
see they loved me. So I'll work to
create love for me from Lori. I might
see a love in her eyes, a warmth, an
attraction for me, a vulnerability
toward me, because I created it there.
I create that look in Lori's eyes by
asking questions sensorily: "Where do
I see that warmth in Lori's eyes?"
First in the left eye. Then I ask the
question of the right eye. What happens to her eyes when she smiles? What
actually is love as it manifests itself
in an eye? It really isn't in the eye
itself. It's all around the eye - the
welling up of tears, the wrinkles a-
round the eye, the light changes. Now
if I pursue this investigation, asking
many more questions, and not just visual
ones, I might have the beginning of a
relationship of loving Lori and caring
about her very much. I'm not dealing
with any of the other obligations yet,
the guilt and the discomfort, just the
love. And I'm working with her eyes
as my choice, hoping it will do for me
what I want it to do. It may not. I
may sit here and at the end of that rehearsal time I may say, "Hey, you know
I liked it, Lori, but I don't feel the
things I want to feel." Then I may
have to boost my choice, add to it or
go for another choice altogether. And
I'm still working for that one element

of caring for her, loving her. <u>One</u>
<u>obligation</u>, <u>one choice</u>, <u>one sensory</u>
<u>approach</u>.

Now while I'm working for my choice in
relation to Lori, Lori exists and anything Lori does will affect me, hopefully, because I'm open to her. This
is the area where most actors go down
the tubes, because they want to act,
they want to behave, they want to feel
what the author tells them to feel.
All I feel is what Lori makes me feel
and what my choice makes me feel. I'm
going to say the lines and I'm going
to ask the sensory questions in between
and include all the life that's going
on in me. That's what I express, the
sum total of the questions and their
responses and all the life that's going
on. In rehearsal you work for your
choice at the cost of the material until you find out if that choice, fully
explored, will complement the material
or not. (End of tape.)

The Rewards of Sense Memory

In order to create an object that does not
exist, it may take you seven hundred questions
before you get the beginnings of a sense of
it. After you become a master craftsman,
through years of hard work and application,
instead of saying in the Second Act transi-
tion, "I will work for my grandmother and I'll
ask how high does she stand in the doorway,
how much of the door does she take up, what
color is her hair, etc.", you will have become so risible and sensorily alive and knowing of your instrument that when you pick up
your script and say, "Okay, in the Second Act

I'm going to work for my grandmother", all you'll do is say, "Grandma!" and it'll all be there. You'll get the same full, complete response from the mere suggestion of the choice that you would have gotten in your first year after asking four hundred questions. Ultimately your instrument becomes so pure and so totally responsive that it asks and answers the questions at the same time. The craft then is no longer a craft, because you have become the totality of it.

PREPARATION

"Methinks I Hear A Cannon"

Acting is ninety-five per cent preparation.
If you are ready to act, then you can.

The Scene: An agent's office in New York City.
An actor is sitting in the waiting room reading the trades. In the inner office the agent
is talking on the phone, ". . . No, . . . I
don't handle any last-minute one-line actors
. . . I don't know any actors who'd take one
line up at Stratford tonight even if it is
Shakespeare!"

At this point, the actor rushes in from the
waiting room and whispers desperately, "I'll
take it! I'll take it!" The agent wraps up
the deal and that same afternoon the actor
finds himself on the train to Stratford.
Like Rodin's Thinker, his head is resting in
his hand, his elbow propped on the window-
sill. He looks deeply into the passing scenery without seeing. His lips move, silently
repeating his one line of dialogue. "Methinks I hear a cannon. . . Methinks I hear
a cannon. . . "

At the same time, he ponders on what to use
for his preparation. He knows he should
start with relaxation, but he must also find
some choices for his role, because he's a
Method actor and wouldn't dream of going on
stage unprepared. "I think I'll use a mi-
graine headache," he decides, "because mi-
graine headaches make me feel rotten. I

want to get that going first and then I'll work
for a bad lung, because that will center me,
make me feel something's really going on inside
Methinks I hear a cannon. . . Methinks I hear a
cannon. . . Now I need one more thing to give m
the spine of the character. I'll work for my
father. I hated my father. That'll give me a
real emotional force. . . Methinks I hear a can
non. . . Methinks I hear a cannon. . . "

He arrives at the theatre. They suit him in
armor and give him a spear. An hour before cur
tain time he is pacing backstage, working on
his preparation and repeating his one line.
They give him the five-minute warning and tell
him where to stand. He takes his position and
continues his diligent preparing. The curtain
goes up. There is a loud cannon blast. He
recoils and exclaims, "WHAT THE HELL WAS THAT!"

Misunderstanding Preparation

This is a classic Method joke known to almost
everyone. It illustrates several important
problems related to people's misconception of
the Method. An actor who doesn't understand
either the purposes or the uses of preparation
makes preparation a thing unto itself. This
is how the Method got its bad reputation. The
Cannon joke shows how an actor can get so involved in extraneous and confused preparation
that the process hinders rather than helps.

What is preparation? Preparation is the work
you do to get you to the point where you can
do your work. Many actors think that is a
specific thing you do to get to a specific
state, but that is only one kind. There are
numerous kinds - lifelong preparations for
your own growth as an artist, instrumental

preparations, daily practice, preparations
for a relationship to another person in a
play, preparations to change your ego-state
and many other kinds. An actor should be
familiar with all forms of readiness besides
the readiness to say the lines.

I used to think that preparation was only a
state that you had to achieve so that you
could act. Certainly that's a creative and
organic form of preparation, but if that's
the only kind you ever learn, then you are
limited to that one state of readiness.
Where do you go from there? AN ACTOR PRE-
PARES - to do what? One preparation you use
may only lead to the next level of preparation. For example, I walk into a theatre to
rehearse a play and I'm tense that day and
insulated and I'm not sensorily alive and
I've had a bad day and I'm protecting myself.
So I might begin with a Relaxation exercise.
Then I'd sensitize and do a Personal Inventory, and then maybe a couple of Vulnerability exercises. Hopefully, by then I'd feel
open and ready to work. The scene obligates
me to be concerned, compassionate, and unable
to help the situation. When I walked into
the theatre, I couldn't have cared less about
anyone. After these initial preparations, I
may still not be compassionate, but I'm ready
now to do a second kind of preparation, which
is to work for choices that might take me to
feeling what the character feels. My first
level of preparation was preparation to prepare.

These two kinds of preparation depend entirely on your daily practice preparations. Are
you practicing daily your Relaxation, Sensitizing, Personal Inventory and Sense Memory
so that when you try to use them, you can?
All of this is based on the philosophy of

BEING. If you don't regularly practice getting to the reality of what is going on in you, then when you start to work, you are not functioning from your true origin. The daily practice of BEING is your instrumental preparation. So Far we've described four kinds of preparation that are implicit just by the actor walking into the theatre for a rehearsal. The nature of your preparation will always be determined by what you need at that moment.

The Cannon story illustrates how an actor often deludes himself into believing that the work he's doing is helping him, when actually that work is only adding to his burden and preventing him from seeing the simplest truths and responding to what he sees and hears. Had the Cannon actor simply listened, he would have heard the cannon and responded honestly to that Instead he had a predetermined concept of the character as being much more complicated than was written and his preparation, rather than leading him to a state of BEING, only fortified his cerebral complexity, taking him farther and farther away from his real obligations.

Many so-called Method actors pay lip service to the craft while their preparations run in paral lel to what they've already decided to do and does not at all influence their resultant be- havior. They'd act the same with or without preparation. That is why many actors, reputed to be Method-trained, turn out performances which are mannered, cliche and predictable.

You must always start first with getting to wha is - here and now - right or wrong for that rol Only in a state of BEING can you really know what you need at that moment and then be able to select the right preparations. If you do no start with the real truth, your own truth, you cannot service the truths in the material. Onl from a state of BEING can you hope to make a connection with your unconscious life.

Begin by BEING

The bedrock of YOU - all of your creativity comes from that. BEING becomes a part of your daily lifetime preparation. BEING is the totality of everything you are, including everything you feel and the expression of that. The following group of exercises relate to BEING and since, that is the first step in the process of preparation, you should most often start there.

1: One-Person BEING

We've already described this exercise in Chapter I, page   . Find your own ways to practice it daily.

2: Two-People BEING

Described in Chapter II, page   . The exercise can best be used as a daily preparation at those times when you are working on a scene with another actor and you meet periodically for rehearsals.

3: Personal Inventories

Described in Chapter I, page   , and Chapter II, page   . Practice it daily as often as you can. Besides asking yourself How Do I Feel and What Do I Want, put special emphasis on Am I Expressing What I Feel and If Not, Why Not, and What Can I Do About It? This last group of questions particularly relates to the obstacles that keep you from expression.

4. The BEING Workout

This exercise is done with a series of changing partners in a group setting, either an acting class or rehearsal group. You can also adapt it for your daily BEING practice by doing it encounter-style with each person you meet, or whenever your common sense tells you it's applicable.

Start by relating to your partner on a here-and-now basis, acknowledging all the distractions that keep you from relating, including your self-consciousness and your concerns outside the relationship. Also deal with obstacl between you and the other person that keep you from BEING with that person, such as your fea your worry about doing the right thing, socia obligation, sexual attraction, hostility, unsaid feelings, repulsion, your impression that the other person expects something from you, lack of interest in the person, etcetera. Unless these things are acknowledged and expressed audibly or semi-audibly, they will preven you from BEING comfortable and organic in you relationship to that person.

Repeat the exercise with each one of your cha ing partners. Each person will present a dif ferent set of obstacles, some less than other Repetition of the BEING Workout builds the ha of eliminating the obstacles that keep you fr being yourself with anyone. The goal is to accept the life that is, no matter what it is and to become more comfortable with uncomfor table feelings. *Once you have acknowledged a expressed the obstacles to BEING, then you ca BE.*

There's a story about an old-school, Russian Jewish actor who visits his friend, an author and says to him, "I don't know. You are a writer and you are sitting down and you are

190

typing something, finishing a script, looking
at the script. You are working, you got
something to look at. A painter, he paints
a picture, he sees his picture. I am working
and I am finished and all I have is spit on
the mirror."

Writers write, painters paint, dancers dance,
but actors sit and drink coffee. Or they
stay in their rooms, like the wistful old
man in the story, practicing the wrong things
and ending up with nothing but spit on the
mirror. There are many reasons why actors
don't commit themselves to preparation as a
way of life, to a daily regimen of practice.
One reason is a lack of knowledge about what
to practice. Acting teachers say, "Go out
and observe." Observe what? How? And how
do you use it? Ignorance of what to work on
leads to the avoidance of work altogether.

Other actors, diligent and dedicated but without solid knowledge of their craft, practice
things that are not helpful to their growth.
Also the lack of a tangible product deters
many an actor from homework, as the old man
complains in the story. At the end of a
practice session, you cannot lay your hands
on your work, on a painting or a statue or a
novel. The loneliness of daily practice is
all the more poignant when there seems to be
no tangible rewards.

But there are rewards. Each day you build a
bank account of skills with which you can create realities and when you get on stage, you
have a great deal more than just spit on the
mirror. There isn't a serious artist in the
world who doesn't spend every day working at
his art. Somerset Maughm used to sit down at
nine o'clock every morning to write and he'd
write his name over and over again until an

idea came to him. He did this for discipline.

JELLYBEAN: DESERT YOUR ART FOR ONE DAY
AND IT WILL DESERT YOU FOR THREE

Daily Practice

Here are some things you should do every day.
You should deal every day with some aspect of
your ability to Relax. You should Sensitize
more than once a day. Do Personal Inventories
as often as you can fit them into your daily
activities. Observation exercises such as
Observe, Wonder, Perceive, The Farmer's Market
etc. Sense Memory daily, with and without objects. All kinds of BEING exercises. Self
Inventories to build up your stockpile of
choices. These exercises and many others
that appear in this book should be practiced
daily by every actor.

Then, of course, as you learn to know your individual needs, you will also use instrumental
exercises daily to overcome those specific
problems.

All the exercises in this chapter can be practiced daily depending on your individual needs
And all of them lead ultimately to the fulfillment of dramatic material as well as expanding
your growth as a person.

There are three major categories of preparatio
and all the exercises in this chapter fall int
one or more of these categories.

1: Instrumental Preparations
    These are all the exercises related to you
    to your living and acting problems. You
    are your instrument. You may have problem

related to tension, fear, inhibition, or insulation. Your preparations in this category will focus on alleviating these and other instrumental problems. The preparations you do in this area are analogous to the scales a concert pianist practices. You exercise to open your instrument, dealing with the obstacles that get in the way of being free and ready to work.

2: Preparations for Relating to People, Objects and Places
These are the exercises that enable you to relate to people outside of yourself and to objects and to your physical environments. Since living and acting are inseparable, you practice in your day-to-day relationships so that you become more observant, sensitized, affectable and responsive to external stimulation. As you are more vulnerable to people, objects and places, you will have more success in using these elements as choices in dramatic material.

3: Preparations for Doing the Role
These are the things that get you ready to do the part, the role, the scene, to fulfill the emotional obligations of the material.

These three categories often depend on one another. It would be impossible to prepare to do the scene if you were not instrumentally ready to work. In the scene you're doing, you might have a lot of difficulty relating to the other character if you have not prepared to relate. Also, the following exercises often overlap each other from one category to the next. You can use many of them for many purposes. For instance, a

Vulnerability Exercise is a part of your instrumental preparation, but you could, at
times, use it specifically to fulfill an emotional obligation in a role or a scene. The
three categories are only to make clear to
you the reasons why you're doing whatever
it is you're doing.

I.   INSTRUMENTAL PREPARATIONS

A.   PREPARATIONS FOR AWARENESS

Awareness is an ongoing process, a daily conditioning. Preparations for elevating your
awareness should become a way of life. The
exercises here are designed to make you more
aware. As you go along, you should discover
and invent more of your own.

5.   The Cluster of Four

For a number of years, I've been starting my
classes every week with The Cluster of Four,
because I've found it's an ideally balanced
group of exercises to begin with. The Cluster
consists of Relaxation (Logey, Tense and Relax
Deep Breathing, Rag Doll, etc.), Sensitizing,
Personal Inventory and What Do I Want, as part
of the Personal Inventory. Chapter II contains full descriptions of all of these. It's
important to say that the sequence of The
Cluster was not arrived at by accident, but
by trial and error and success. First of all,
you deal with your physical tension so that
you can then Sensitize, raising your senses
to higher levels of sensitivity. Then you go
on to find out how you feel and what you want
through Personal Inventory.

6. Super Consciousness

Start with an arbitrary decision to become
super conscious, super aware of everything
going on around you in all five sensory
areas. You decide, "I'm now going to be
super conscious. I'm going to hear every
possible sound so that my ears can record
the most obvious sounds down to the most
subtle. I'm going to see, smell, taste,
touch everything. I see all the fruit and
papers on the table and I devour it through
all my five senses, ingesting every detail
like a sponge."

Do it for ten or fifteen minutes. It's a
somewhat unnatural exercise in that your
acute observations usurp a more natural moment-to-moment flow of life and you may not
be able to relate to anyone while you're
doing it, unless that person becomes the
object of your Super Consciousness and then
you will relate to him quite unnaturally.
However, daily repetition of Super Consciousness automatically raises your level of
awareness.

7. Farmer's Market

In Chapter II this exercise is explained
thoroughly. We remind you here that it applies to your instrumental preparation for
awareness.

8. Observe, Wonder and Perceive

Also described in Chapter II. Actors are
notoriously self-involved and narcissistic.
This simple exercise is very difficult for
many actors, because the habit of being aware
and observant of someone other than yourself
often comes hard. But with regular practice,

Observe, Wonder and Perceive - as with all
these exercises - transcends from a deliberate decision to become a part of your life.

Dialogue on Craft

Eric: How many times have you heard me say,
       "The craft is designed to do away with
       itself."?

Joan: Many, many times. And I've experienced
       it, because in this last play I was in,
       I certainly wasn't taking notes on each
       of these processes during my perfor-
       mances, but in retrospect when I came
       offstage I could define for you as on
       a road map many of these things that
       were going on automatically while I
       was tending to the play. Simultaneous
       habits. Personal Inventory was going
       on all the time in the lines and in
       between the lines. Sensory Awareness.
       Vulnerability. My observation, wonder-
       ment, perception were constant. All
       of these exercises weren't exercises
       anymore. They were me.

Eric: As a result of conditioned responses
       through practice. Good point. Now to
       make the point very clear, the transi-
       tion from an exercise to a way of life
       relates to what I just said - The craft
       is designed to do away with itself. If
       you do these exercises often enough,
       repeatedly, in your day to day living,
       in your acting, in your rehearsals, in
       your life, they become a part of the
       moment-to-moment fabric of your BEING.
       They become you.

9.   Sensory Inventory

We go into this exercise in full detail in
Chapter II.   Sensory Inventory is the investigation of all your senses and what makes
them work, how they are affected by external
stimuli.   An important point - as you repeat
the exercise day by day, your sensory acuity
grows and more and more parts of each sense
begin to function.   So it's an endless investigation that stimulates an increasingly
higher and higher level of sensory awareness.

10.   Sense Memory

This exercise is one of the best kinds of
stimulation for awareness.   Do a sense memory exercise every day of your life from
fifteen minutes to three hours.   Spend as
much time as you can on it.   Sensory training progressively heightens your accessibil-
ity,sensorily and emotionally.   While you
are practicing, encouraging your senses to
respond to imaginary stimuli, you will be
astonished at the steady expansion of your
awareness.

11.   Sensuality

This is a three-part exercise you can do
either alone or in a group.   I've found it
to be effective following The Cluster of
Four.   The first part has to do with sensuality related to your own body.   The second
part is sensuality toward inanimate objects
and the third part, which you would omit if
you were doing it alone, is sensuality related to other people.

Start with the first part, touching yourself
with your hands all over your body.   Sensorily and sensually feel the shapes and

contours of your body, your muscularity, the
varying textures of your skin and clothing.
Encourage your body to respond to the touch
of your hands, besides being aware of what
your hands are feeling, so that tactilely you
are responding on both ends. Allow your body
to find its own sensual rhythm and movement
as you explore it, tasting yourself, smelling
yourself and hearing your sensual sounds.
Help yourself to make sounds that come out of
your feeling of sensuality and let the rhythmic movements of your body flow together with
your sounds to create your own beat. Include
your genital areas and any sexual response
that is part of the sensuality. This first
section of the exercise builds slowly until
your entire body is involved and moving -
your neck, your head, your shoulders, arms,
wrists, ankles, knees, as well as the pelvis
area.

Then you go to the second part, to objects.
Sensually relate to the wall, the floor, the
rug, the chair, any objects in the room, such
as a purse or jacket or book or an ashtray.
Expose all parts of your body to the object
so that your entire body relates to it sensually. If it's a small object, move it around
on your face, in and around your mouth, under
your arms, your chest, your stomach, inside
your thighs down to the bottoms of your feet.
If it's the rug or the wall, make total contact, front and back, letting every contour
of your body touch the wall and again, as in
the first part of the exercise, stimulate a
rhythmic movement, your own sensual beat, as
you taste and smell and listen to the fric-
tion of your body against the object.

Then you go to people. You might start by
just touching each other's hands or put your
cheek up against a thigh or bury your face in

someone's hair and smell it, taste it and
let it tickle your skin. You might stand
back to back and make rhythmic contact and
sensually enjoy the sounds and movements.
Encourage yourself to taste and smell and
touch things that you might conventionally
avoid, such as smelling someone's shoe or
tasting a toe or chewing on the strap of a
handbag or chair. Sometimes you do this
with two people, sometimes three or four or
six. Sometimes it culminates in a whole
mound of people sensualizing with one another.

The exercise often stimulates a degree of
sexuality, which is all right if you are
using it as a preparation for sexuality.
However, its main purpose is to increase
your awareness and the sensory availability
of your entire body. A variation of the
exercise is called Primal Sensuality, which
is done the same way except that you approach
it from the beginning with a larger commitment to be more animal and primitive in both
your movements and sounds. This variation
serves to break down barriers more quickly.

There are endless exercises for awareness
besides the ones suggested here. Any one of
these could branch off into a whole group of
exercises. As you work daily you will come
upon many things that work for you particularly and these will grow into your own repertoire of awareness preparations.

B. EGO PREPARATIONS

As an actor at school I was known as "the
brooding Dane," because I was so often depressed. For years, as I worked profession-
ally, I seldom felt I had the right to be

heard, the right to take the time to prepare when other people were waiting for me to start the reading, the right to stop in the middle of a take and do it over. I did what most actors do: I did what I thought was expected of me at the cost of what I really had to offer.

It was not until I started teaching that I found ways to help myself as an actor, because as a teacher I could see objectively, while dealing with other actors, how important it was to isolate and define this whole area of the actor's ego and how it affects his work. There are good race horses that lose the race because they don't get out of the gates. As a teacher I noticed that very talented people, even the most talented people, often had difficulty getting out of their gates, getting beyond their depressions and insecurities, so that they could use their craft and function creatively. Once they started to act, their talent would sometimes carry them through, but it wasn't something they could count on. I saw that it was at this beginning point, this pre-starting point, where many actors would get stuck, and rather than find ways to help themselves, they'd panic and fake it, imposing behavior to meet the theatrical demands.

I observed that actors suffer from a variety of ego-ailments, insidious demons that whisper to them, "You're not good enough. . . Nobody wants you. . . You're too old. . . You're too young. . . You're not good-looking enough. . . You don't have enough talent. . . You never went to college. . . You're a fool to keep trying. . . " In the work we did in class, the whole concept of the actor's ego-state became more and more important as part of his instrumental preparation. I took some common

Group Sensuality. The main purpose is to increase your awareness and the sensory availability of your entire body.

sensical exercises and devised others, inventing some fortunate accidents that happened during scenes and during individual work and created an area which I call Ego Preparations.

There must be at least seventy-vive exercises in this area alone, which we practice in class and which actors who've studied with me use in their professional work. All of the exercises help the actor to change his ego-state to a better ego-state in which he can feel like working and allow himself to succeed. The exercises have many different emphases to match whatever the ego-difficulty is at that moment. When you feel insecure about your ability to act, you can do an ego exercise affirming the solidity of your craft (Count Your Craftual Blessings). If you are ready to work, but you feel physically insecure, disgusted with how you look, there are exercises for raising your physical self-acceptance. If you feel negative and depressed, you can do any number of Positivity exercises. If you're afraid to be heard making large statements, you can choose from many kinds of large-commitment exercises to help yourself. The selection is limitless, depending on what you need.

Besides supporting your readiness to work, you can also use an ego exercise as a choice to fulfill the emotional obligations in a scene from a play. If you want to feel bad, but that night you're feeling good, you might reverse one of the ego preparations to bring yourself down. Or maybe you're feeling neutral, not depressed, but not excited either. You might first want to do an ego preparation to lift your state to something more alive and inspired so that you can then sink down into the required depression, but still have exciting impulses.

Ego preparations are an integral part of your instrumental preparation, because without sufficient acceptance of yourself, you cannot reach your talent, no matter how much talent you have.

12.   Get A Sense Of What You Used To Be

This is a morale-building exercise. Often an actor will despair at how far he has to go down the road. "Look how far I have to go!" This exercise says to him, "Look how far you've come!" He gets a perspective on his growth over the past three to five years.

There are two ways you can do it. First, you can simply remember how you were three to five years ago, how you related to people, how you handled certain situations, the acting jobs you had and how you approached your craft. You can either think about these things or talk about them to yourself or to a group. The second way is to do an affective memory exercise and truthfully re-experience yourself at that time. This way is more time-consuming and complicated, but it has the added benefit of giving you a kind of behavior that you could use in a script.

13.   Take Your Due

Most effective done in a group or with another person. Express out loud in words and action all the positive things you feel you have coming to you. Ask for what you want from various people around you. "Joe, I want you to pay more attention to me. Sue, I want you to take me more seriously. I want you all to stop talking while I'm doing this exercise." Talk about areas in which you feel you've been mis-

understood and you haven't received your
due. "None of you know this, but I'm a
terrific photographer and I paint well and
some day I'm going to be recognized for
the actor I am. Peter, you think I'm overly
critical of you, but I really expect a lot
of you because you're very talented and
that's why I demand so much. I want all of
you to know that I'm filled with love. I
have a lot of love to give and I want you
to be open to accept it."

As you do this exercise repeatedly, your
trust grows. You gain confidence in your
ability to make your own statement. Remember to make your statement physically as
well, standing up to your full height, taking up your rightful space, allowing yourself to be flamboyant in your gestures, if
you wish.

Of course, there are some actors who misin-
terpret any exercise. I had a student once,
a husky young man named Mickey. Everytime
I gave him this exercise, he'd systematically tear up the theatre, flinging chairs from
wall to wall, ripping pillows. He even frac-
tured his hand once ramming it through a
door. I finally decided to give my theatre
its due and stopped asking him to do this
exercise.

14. Sense Of Worth

You can do it alone or in a group. The purpose is to put you in touch with your worthy
accomplishments. People often tend to mini-
mize or forget things which they've worked
very hard to accomplish. Express all your
abilities and successes and in so doing you
will bring to the surface a sense of worth
that you may not have started with.

5. Don't Care

Do it alone or in a group. You say, "I don't care about ____. I don't care that ____. I don't care for ____. I couldn't care less that ......" A sample: "I don't care what goes on in Washington. I don't care about trivial gossip. I don't care what Betty just said about Jean. I don't care if I'm not always understood. I used to care about that a lot, but I don't anymore. I don't care as much about being good as I used to. I don't care for a lot of people. etc., etc."

This exercise allows you to clean house mentally and frees you from concerns so that you can relate to what you really do care about. Sometimes a conglomeration of concerns makes you feel oppressed and weighted down. Deliberate expurgation of these things you don't care about can lessen your load and put your ego in a different place so that you can work.

6. Positivity and Validation

There are two ways to approach the Positivity exercise. You can start with whatever positive impulses you really feel and verbalize them. "I kind of like being here. It's a nice place. I like some of the people here. I feel physically good. . ." Build from there, looking for more and more positive things to get involved in. If that leads you to more and more positive feelings, good. If it doesn't, you can then begin to exaggerate, being arbitrarily positive, until you feel more positive.

The second approach is the way you start the exercise when you are feeling so negative that even the thought of being positive is impossible. You can then begin the exercise

206

with the deliberate decision to exaggerate,
even to lie. You make an arbitrary commitment to say only positive things about everything you see, hear, taste, smell and touch.
"This is a beautiful theatre. I love the
color of the walls. (The walls may be dung
brown, but say it anyway.) All those beautiful people are out there, paying attention
to me and sending me signals of love. I
feel terrific. I feel overwhelmed with creativity, etc." Hopefully, you will connect
at some point with the seeds of your buried
positivity.

Validation is a variation of the Positivity
exercise. You go around the room and express supportive, validating thoughts about
each person. "Corinne, I think you're a
very warm and giving person. I'm glad you're
here. John, I love the way you're dressed
tonight. Your concern with the way you look
has really grown. Danny, you're super talented. Allen, your sense of truth is marvelous
In other words, you give out sincere compli-
ments and by honestly validating others, you
begin to feel better about yourself, thereby
changing a negative ego-state to a positive
one.

17. Fun Exercises

Stimulate your own sense of fun in any way
that you can. Get up there and be a baggy
pants clown. Imitate a rooster. Walk a-
round like a chicken and cockadoodledoo.
Make funny faces and crazy sounds at everybody. Be as silly as you can, a "silly-
dilly." Distort your body into ridiculous
positions and talk jibberish to people in
the room. If that doesn't make you feel
better, nothing will.

18. Comparative Ego

Do this exercise silently so as not to alienate anyone. Find in each person around you the things that make you feel better off than he or she, whether it's physical, intellectual, emotional, financial, theatrical. You think to yourself things like, "I'm glad I have enough money so I don't have to scrounge for it the way Jane does. . . " "I'm better looking than Harry and I'm younger." "I've done much more work than most of these people." "Who here knows more than I do about acting?" Do the Comparative Ego until you feel better and you can do it anywhere, on a movie set, on the street, in a class, at a party.

19. Make Yourself Beautiful

This exercise deals with your physical self and you use the sensory process to create a greater sense of yourself. Start with what is, defining what you really feel good about, even if it's only one thing. Maybe you have a good bust. Parade it around. Relate to it with pride. Emphasize and magnify it, feeling your sense of power in that area. Strut around the room and intensify your somewhat positive feelings about yourself into extremely positive feelings, finding as many real things as possible.

The next step is imaginary. Sensorily endow yourself with imaginary attributes. Caress your face and endow it with satin skin, petal-soft. Surround yourself with delectable odors emanating from your body. Make yourself bigger where you want to be bigger and smaller where you want to be smaller. Look into a real or imaginary mirror and create a dazzling reflection with sparkle in your eyes and highlights in your hair.

20. Take-Over or Evangelist

This is a large-commitment type of exercise
designed to excite yourself and others, to
get your adrenalin going. It's excellent
for passive people, for soft-spoken and shy
actors and actresses, whose egos need a
boost. You simply make a large commitment
to "taking over" a group of people and like
a circus barker you sell them anything from
an idea to a health product to religion to
smoke-colored glasses for looking at eclipses.
Capture their attention and hold it through
your own excitement. Lecture to them, preach,
chant, become an evangelist, a revivalist.
Even if the exercise feels uncomfortable at
first and out of character for you, jump in
and do it arbitrarily. In a short time you
will be caught up in the momentum and it will
carry you along. Your ego will become bou-
yant.

21. Magic Pocket

A marvelous ego exercise, which depends on
your imagination. You can do it through a
simple suggestion or through sense memory.
Imagine that in one of your pockets you have
something magnificent. A contract to a studio for seven years with astronomically es-
calating salaries. A telegram saying that
you've won the Academy Award. Keys to a
Rolls Royce parked outside. A wallet that
never runs out of money. A letter from someone you've always loved and don't see anymore,
asking you to join that person on an ocean
voyage. You have in your pocket anything you
can imagine being there either in reality or
symbolically. The magic aspect of the exercise is vital. You must encourage yourself
to believe in the magic. Walk around with
your hand in your pocket or patting the

outside of it and allow the belief to grow
until you feel totally in possession of the
most important thing in your life.

22. Yeah! Yeah!

"yeah. . . Yean. . . YEah. . . YEAh!. . .
YEAH! YEAH!! YEAH!!!!!" Starting small
and building to a crescendo, you say the one
word over and over, bigger and bigger until
it becomes a gigantic shout from the soles
of your feet to the top of your head. The
force of that positivity will fill your whole
being and excite everyone around you. The
exercise makes you want to go out and push
down walls.

23. Feel and Affirm Self
(Superman and Superwoman)

Make physical contact with your body, touching
your muscles, whether you're a man or a woman.
Press, knead and pat those parts where you
feel strong and encourage the strength to grow
in those parts and circulate and course through
the rest of you. Flex your muscles, strut,
pose, stand erect, squeeze the muscles of your
thighs as you stride along and with each step
become aware of your external and internal
strength. You can accompany your movements
with sounds, either verbal or nonverbal, in a
simplistic way, such as, "I AM. I FEEL. I'M
STRONG. I FEEL MY POWER." You will experience a growing affirmation of yourself.

Since you are one of a kind, unique unto yourself, your ego concerns will be individual
and you will learn what you need in this area
as you become more aware of all of your preparational needs. The exercises here cover a
variety of ego areas. Invent your own exercises. Fashion your own tools for dealing

with your ego. In order to act you must always feel that you have the right to be where
you are and to do what you are doing.

C. PREPARATIONS FOR VULNERABILITY

Dialogue on Vulnerability

Eric: You know that area I've talked to you
about, separating the craft into two
major categories, the impressive and
the expressive?

Joan: Yes, yes.

Eric: Vulnerability definitely relates to
the impressive category. Preparation
for vulnerability is another area,
like the Ego area, that I found, in
working with actors and working as an
actor myself, was very important. If
ninety-eight per cent of acting is
preparation, the emphasis must be on
preparation, because if you are prepared to act, then you can and if you
are not prepared to act, then you
can't. The exercises for vulnerability stimulate your ability to be affected and risible. All of the exercises in this category make you more
sensitive to real and imaginary stimuli. Now that's a very important
point. . . real and imaginary. . .
because if you become more available
to being affected by more things, you
will increase your threshold of availability, increase your vulnerability
on a day-to-day living level and on a
here-an-now acting level. Do you know
what I mean?

Joan: I sure do.

Eric: If you get more vulnerable as the days
go by, you are affected by more existing things that were always there. And
also, as you become more risible and
affectable and vulnerable, you are affected by the imaginary things which
you suggest, create or work for. So
vulnerability is a monster of an important area in your preparation, because it makes you ready to be affected.
For example, in class last night, you
remember? - I was talking to Lori and
I said to her you must first get to the
stage of vulnerability and surrender to
it before you can play an uptight bitch,
and she understood that. A lot of actresses wouldn't understand that. They
would start right away to work for the
end result, the uptight bitch, closing
all the doors.

Joan: That's right. The uptight bitch might
be uptight, because she's afraid of her
vulnerability underneath. You gotta
get that. You gotta find out what's
underneath the uptight thing on top.
Another thing is that this area of vulnerability is particularly embarrassing
for actors to work on, because it feels
squishy. It feels naked and unacty.
It feels defenseless. And there's that
traditional thing about the "professional", you know - you go in and say your
jokes and get your money. And even some
sophisticated actors, who are sensitive
people, do not allow themselves to be
vulnerable on the set, on the job. It
can be risky and they'd rather keep
control of themselves, because they
think that is what a professional is.

When an actor really works in this area of vulnerability, he's not going to look professional in that slick sense of the word. He's going to look rough and bumpy.

Eric: Yeah, sometimes the red balls are all rolling in one direction and you're the white ball rolling the other way. You're a target, but you've got to do the work you have to do in order to do the kind of work you want to do. The results of your work on vulnerability, the results in terms of your performance, will far surpass the results of the conventional actor who says his jokes. They may laugh at you on the set or be embarrassed for you, avoid you even, but when they see your work on the screen, the laughing stops. So be the white ball and keep rolling in the direction your preparation takes you.

Joan: Right! Absolutely.

Eric: I want to say one other thing. Last night in class, Joy said to me, "I don't want to feel. I don't want to be affected. I don't want to go through it!" It's true, it's uncomfortable, sometimes painful. As you grow and feel more, it is very threatening, very intimidating, expecially if your conditioning has been to protect yourself against feeling. But as I said to Joy last night and again and again, it's the truth, you gotta go through the thickest part of the woods in order to get out of the woods. You can stand, looking into the woods all your life and never go through them

213

and never get to the other side. This
applies to <u>any</u> area, much less vulnerability.

Joan: Wait a minute. If you're going to be
a bank teller, then it's okay to look
through the woods and not go through
them.

Eric: I don't know. My feeling is that I
think you can enjoy life more by functioning in terms of what you really
feel, all your sensitivities, even if
you're a bank teller.

Joan: But with an actor it's mandatory.

Eric: I don't think a bank teller's liveli-
hood depends on it as an actor's does.
However, opening up, being vulnerable
and experiencing life on a higher and
fuller level is better for everybody,
whatever you do.

24. Group Vulnerability

Vulnerability means being open to all kinds of
emotions, not just the serious, sad things or
the things you're ashamed to expose, but also
the frivolous feelings, and areas of fun and
humor. There are two ways to do the Group
Vulnerability. One individual in the group
can talk about an experience that happened to
him or her, sharing that experience with the
group. It should be an experience that is
filled with strong emotional impulses and
hopefully the group will identify with that
vulnerability and as more individuals share
their experiences, the atmosphere in the room
becomes progressively more sensitive and affectable. This is an excellent exercise for
either a classroom or a rehearsal, because it

makes the group ready to go on either to more
preparational exercises or to dealing with
the responsibilities in a piece of material.
When it's done in a professional rehearsal
setting, it helps if the director leads off
with a vulnerable experience of his own,
modelling a willingness to be open.

Another way is to have the group work by
themselves simultaneously and individually.
Each person works privately for his own
choices and the vulnerable responses are in-
fectious, like laughter or tears. The emotion in the room has a snowball effect, feeding on itself and promoting a higher degree
of vulnerability.

25. Pique and Expose Needs

You can do a semi-audible monologue to yourself expressing your needs. "What do I
need? Well, I need to work more often. I
need more money. I need to have some of the
things I've always wanted. I want not to be
alone anymore. I wish I had more hair. I
want to be thinner. I wish I knew if I were
going to succeed. . ." The needs you express will kick off other areas of vulnerability. For instance, not having some of the
material things you've always wanted might
make you very sad. And besides pathos you
might also find some humor in your needs.

Another way to pique and expose needs is to
work for a stimulus, objects which represent
needs, a place you've been in and long for,
a person you don't see anymore but are still
in love with, a fur coat you can't afford,
your dream car. Working for these kinds of
things should produce a chain reaction leading to other vulnerabilities.

Another way is to express out loud to another person or to a group all the things you need, including what you need from them. "I really need to be good in this play. I need to feel that everybody here likes me and accepts me. I want you to think I'm talented. I need to feel important here." You can also include any one-to-one feelings of need towards anyone in the group.

The hope is that if you truly pique your needs, whatever they are, they will give way to all the other areas of vulnerability surrounding each need. When you deal with the nucleus of something, the related parts of it become available to you and your vulnerability takes on complex dimension.

26. Evocative Words

This exercise came out of a happy accident, as many exercises have. I was working with an actress named Carey. She was sitting on the stage doing an individual exercise. I'd asked her to tell us about a meaningful experience in hopes of her being emotionally affected. She started talking about something that happened to her in school. As I watched her, I saw that she was reporting the experience and her obligation to be understood by us was taking precedence over the impact of the story on her. I stopped her and said, "Don't tell us the story, Carey. Just say single words that relate to the experience." She started saying words connected to that time and that place. After just a few words, she became affected emotionally. As she continued saying words, the emotional life was fuller and fuller. So I started experimenting with other actors and found this exercise very useful and successful.

You can do it by yourself or in front of a

group. You can do it anywhere at any time.
It's a marvelous exercise because you can
use it in many ways - for vulnerability, for
a preparation before going on stage to get
into the right mood, or as a specific choice
in a scene. Think of an experience in your
life that was very meaningful. Start recalling the experience verbally by saying
words related to that time and place and all
the elements involved, such as the people,
what they were wearing, the objects around,
sounds, weather. Say the single words or
brief phrases audibly or semi-audibly. For
instance, something happened to you in a
park. You met with someone you loved and
you were full of hope about the relationship,
but the other person wanted to end it and
you were shocked and deeply hurt. You might
start by saying, "Park. Bench. The trees
around me. Children playing. Carousel music. Balloon. Excitement. Blue sky. He's
coming. Blond. Graduation ring. Damp
ground. Serious eyes. Hi. Love you. No.
Please. Don't say that. No sound. Lost.
Sitting on the bench. Alone. Late. Cold
. . ."

If you're pleased with the level of vulnerability you feel, fine. If you want to a-
chieve a higher level of it, go on to another
experience and repeat the process. It does
not have to be the same kind of experience.
It can be something fun or nostalgic.

Besides its preparational value, you can use
this exercise as a choice in a scene to fulfill the emotional obligation of the material. By saying meaningful words to yourself
in between the lines, you can stimulate the
emotional life required by that section of
the play.

217

27. Sensory Choice

Simply work for a choice through the use of
sense memory, using an object which stimulates
in you a high degree of emotional vulnerability.

28. Affection, Tenderness and Love

Express verbally your feelings of affection,
tenderness and love towards the people in your
group. It can be done in a classroom group, a
rehearsal gathering or on a film set with the
people around you, who don't necessarily have
to know that you're doing this exercise. Look
around the room and find the things that exist
which really make you feel affectionate and
tender, and start there. Express your feelings audibly or semi-audibly, whichever the
situation dictates. "I really like you, John.
I feel tremendous affection for you and I'm
very attracted to you. Carol, your being here
means a lot to me. I feel you're really supportive of me and encouraging." You can expand the expression of your tenderness and
love to things outside of the group, people
in your personal life. "I'm so in love with
Mark. Last night in the restaurant his eyes
were full of concern for me. And I adore my
children. I'm overwhelmed with feeling when
I see them. And my dog - oh, my dog, I'm
crazy about my dog. He's so cute." The exercise stimulates internally the feelings of
affection, tenderness and love which lead to
a level of vulnerability.

29. Fear, Love and Hate

You can do it semi-audibly, but it's better if
you do it out loud to a group or another person. Talk about your fears and the things you
love and hate, tossing them all together like
an emotional salad. In this exercise you're
not committed to just your fears or your loves

or hates. You can mix them around. Be sure
you take responsibility for expressing what
you feel about each thing rather than just
reporting. And ultimately you will pique
meaningful emotional responses to things
that are deeply important in your life.

30. Ask For Help

There are two ways to do this one. The first
way is simply to say, "Help me. Please help
me." Repeat the phrase over and over, either
alone or preferably to a group, until that one
phrase reaches down into you and touches your
needs. The second way is to ask for some
specific kind of help related to a real need.
"Would you please help me overcome my laziness
Would you call me every day and make sure I'm
rehearsing? Would you help me by telling me
when I'm hostile, because I don't know when
I am and I really need not to be."

31. Imaginary Monologue

I started using the Imaginary Monologue about
eleven years ago, but at first I called it
the Steering Wheel Monologue, because I used
to do it driving my car. I'd drive along and
I'd always be telling people off, having imaginary confrontations demanding what was
rightfully mine or I'd tell someone how much
I really cared, pouring out affection that
in reality would be embarrassing to us both.
I introduced it to the class after I'd discovered something about myself - that I did
not have to face the consequences of the
other person being there, and that it always
stimulated in me some kind of emotional life.

Talk to someone who is not now here as if
that person were really here, talking about
things that would be either difficult or impossible for you to say if the person were

219

really here. You will elicit meaningful, gut-
level kinds of emotional investments in your
relationship to the imaginary person.

Imaginary Monologue can serve many purposes.
You can use it to stimulate any kind of emotional response you want as a choice in a
scene or as a preparation before a scene. If
you're doing it for Vulnerability, stress the
areas that are emotionally meaningful to you,
creatively leading yourself into places that
stimulate in you a high degree of vulnerability. You can talk to somebody you're in love
with or somebody who is dead, a parent or
grandparent or any significant person.

32.   Abandonment Exercises for Vulnerability

The Abandonment Exercise was described in
Chapter II as an antidote to tension, but
this type of exercise can be used for many
purposes. Because it is largely expurgative,
it often brings up a flow of emotionality
which leaves you shaky and rumbly inside -
in other words, vulnerable. You can choose
from several types of Abandoment besides the
basic one.

Primitive Abandonment has more form and order,
because it begins with a basic primitive ryth-
mical beat, which you start arbitrarily, encouraging your body to move like a Watusi
warrior and your throat to emit groans and
percussive sounds. Allow your movements and
sounds to build until you experience a kind
of break-through, a climax of primitive release.

Mini-Abandonment is the public version of the
regular abandonment. Use it at those times
when you can't really go all the way in your
environment. Find a place off by yourself
somewhere, in a corner, behind a flat. Do

"Talk about someone who is not now here as if that person were really here." — Meredith McRae doing imaginary monologue.

the Abandonment on a more internal level,
allowing the sounds to come out, but less
vocally. Tense and relax all your muscles
violently, convulsively and repeatedly until the purge begins.

Flip Out is just that. Go crazy. Flamboy-
antly and hugely expurgate all your emotional
energies, all your joy, hate, love, rage,
frustration. The Flip Out is done verbally,
vocally and physically.

Exorcism - Use the physical gesture of pushing away from you and vocal expressions such
as Get Out! Get out of my life! Get away
from me! Leave me alone! Violently rid
yourself of all the people and things which
are suppressing you. Sometimes you might
find yourself doing battle with an abstract
demon, such as Fear.

D. PREPARATIONS FOR THE IMAGINATION

Everybody has an imagination. Somewhere.
Of some kind. Children's imaginations are
available and usable, but as we grow older,
things happen to us which create membranes
that contain and subordinate the imagination.
Because of the responsibilities of life and
because our society does not encourage us to
pretend and to play, even frowns on it,
("That isn't adult, that's childish.") our
imaginations go to sleep.

An actor's talent is very dependent on his
ability to imagine. You must not only work
on your imagination when you have to use it
for a play or a film, but you must also work
on it as part of your daily living preparations, finding all kinds of organized and
unorganized exercises to stimulate it and

stretch it. Start from your stretch point and
go further, expanding your belief that anything
is imaginatively possible. There are no boundaries. Within reality there are boundaries,
but you don't have boundaries to your imagination and you shouldn't make any.

The work you do every day of your life, the
day after day living preparation we've talked
about at the beginning of this chapter, must
include preparations for your imagination.
They must go hand-in-hand with all the other
kinds, the ego preparations, the sensitizing
and sense memory and vulnerability. All the
exercises here and the ten thousand more that
you imaginatively invent should be used for
stretching your imagination.

JELLYBEAN: THE CHILD IS ALIVE IN ALL OF US,
        ASLEEP IN SOME OF US, BUT ALIVE

33. Pretend: Self and Two-People

Either by yourself or with another person,
silently or out loud, pretend whatever pleases
you to pretend, as a child would. Maybe you
are in a forest surrounded by trees and animal
and flowers. When I'm driving on the freeway
coming home from work, I pretend I'm going on
a long trip across the country and I'm consid-
ering where I'll stop for the night. I look
at fancy hotels and pretend I'm driving a Roll
Royce.

When you're working by yourself, try talking
out loud and going through some physical actions to support the pretend circumstances.
Do the exercise five minutes a day or as long
as a whole day, actually venturing out into
the real world pretending to be the rich lady,
talking to real estage agents about buying
this or that mansion, letting them show you

the properties. Imagine how the rich lady
might respond and allow your imagination to
stimulate your behavior. Or be a tramp for
a day, wearing smelly old clothes and hanging around the Skid Row area.

Two-People Pretend is a good preparation for
a scene or to get a relationship going with
another actor. It's also good just to have
fun with, besides the basic purpose of
stretching your imagination. Pretend anything together. For example, you're on an
ocean cruise, sitting in deck chairs talking
about what you'll see and do when you reach
your destination. Or that you and your acting partner have been living together a long
time and you're arguing about your relationship. Both actors should take the initiative
to feed the reality with more and more imaginary circumstances and physical actions.

Although Pretend is not a sense memory exercise, the spinning of pretense often leads
to the seeing, hearing, tasting, feeling and
smelling of those objects and elements that
you're pretending. Pretend can even be used
as a choice in a scene. Joan used it in a
film where she had to gaze proudly at a ridiculous centerpiece in the middle of a
dining table and say, "That's the prettiest
centerpiece I've ever made!" She pretended
it was an Oscar Award and was filled with
effusive joy.

34. Story Telling

Story telling is an ancient art. People use
it for the passing on of history, for sharing
of wisdom and information, or for entertain-
ment to pass the time. In my work with actors I've found several types of story telling exhilerating to the imagination.

<u>Make Up Weird, Outlandish Stories</u> - Do it a-
lone or in a group, silently, semi-audibly or
out loud. "I was eating a hot dog and suddenly I heard a tiny voice, 'Please don't eat me
until I tell you my story.' And the hot dog
told me it had been an orphan. . . etc., etc."
The less conventional the story and the more
chances the teller takes, the better the exercise for the imagination. Remove all boundary
lines of logic. You don't have to make sense.
Start anywhere and go anywhere. The end of
the story does not have to resemble the beginning or have any of the elements you started
with.

<u>Group Story Telling</u> - With or without a mod-
erator, a group of people spin a tale. One
person begins telling a story and at an exciting point, the next person picks it up and
takes it in his or her own direction. "I
heard the footsteps - step by step - coming
closer to the door. I was terrified. The
door slowly opened and in came. . . " The
next person might say, "A huge box of sal-
tines and a glass of milk. And I knew I'd
forgotten my bedtime snack. . . "

35. Essences and Abstracts

A party game. It's important in all of these
imagination exercises to make them fun and
game-like rather than arduous intellectual
feats, because the imagination has its roots
in the unconscious and will flow most freely
when you are relaxed and light-hearted.

The group selects one person, the Questioner,
to leave the room, because the Questioner
must not know who is chosen as the subject
of the game. The group chooses their subject
and the Questioner returns and asks questions
about the person's essences and abstracts.

"What kind of flower does this person have the essence of? What kind of weather? What color would this person be if he or she were an abstract color? What kind of food? What period of history? What character in history embodies the essence of this person? What kind of architecture? What kind of music? What time of day? What kind of odor? What metal?" . . . and so forth.

The Questioner continues until he thinks he can guess the Subject and it's surprising how accurate he often is.

36. Frontis Exercise

The name comes from an actress named Frontis who brought it into my class. It's a group exercise and essentially non-verbal, although as it gathers momentum, sounds may come forth. One person begins it with some kind of real or abstract movement - for instance, conducting a symphony orchestra, standing up tall and moving the arms and the head like Toscanini. After a minute or two, a second person takes over the conducting movement, almost instantaneously changing it to some other form, such as a beautiful big butterfly sailing around the room. The first person sits down. After another couple of minutes, a third person takes over the butterfly and modifies it into something else. The movements can be either real or abstract. Even though they don't necessarily have to resemble something, they should not be without form and some kind of rhythm. The exercise continues in round robin style, the first person picking up the movement from the last person.

37. Fantasies

Fantasies do not have to have any kind of logic or story. They can be formless, fragments of impulses that you don't even understand yourself. They can be verbal or non-vergal or fantasy gibberish. They often engage your wish-fulfillment, your dreams and desires. Involving yourself in fantasies will endlessly enrich your imagination. Daydreaming, nigh dreaming, sexual fantasies, fantasizing with another person, having fantasies about everyone around you, and any other ways you find - explore your world of fantasy!

Exposing yourself to the variety of other people's imaginations helps to expand your own. You can use the group as a barometer to see if your imagination gets stuck, repeating the same pedestrian patterns.

Make Up Fantasy Stories About Objects Around You - Alone or in a group, looking around you, choose an object, maybe the chair in your breakfast room - and make up a fantasy story about it. "That chair belonged to a man by the name of Peter Venton. This man lived in a country village outside of London and he made that chair himself, for his father, who died before receiving it. Peter Venton got so attached to that chair he would sit in no other. He'd stroke the arms as he sat there, which is why the arms are so shiny now, and he'd talk to it. And the scrapes and scratches near the bottom are from his dragging the chair around, because he eventually got so attached to it. . . ", and so on. Use any kind of objects, animate, inanimate, outdoors, indoors. Let your imagination take you on a trip.

<u>Tell An Exciting Story About Yourself</u> - Alone
or in a group, using facts or fiction or a
combination of both, tell an experience you
had (or didn't have), emphasizing all the exciting, adventuresome aspects. Enlarge the
suspense, enhance the romance. This is a
good ego preparation besides a stimulant to
your imagination.

<u>Look At Someone And Supply Imaginary Gaps</u>
This one can be done alone. Choose a person anywhere you are - in a rehearsal group,
a restaurant, a park - and make up a story.
"That person is a circus performer and has
just recently broken away from the circus
and is trying to make a life in the city.
He doesn't have any money and he's desperate.
He's here in this place killing time while
waiting to go see about a job. . . etc., etc."
It's not an observation exercise or a deductive process. Just start with a person
and let your imagination run wild.

38. Children's Games

Red Light, Green Light, Statues, Hide and
Seek, Be Animals, Object Charades (take the
form of an inanimate object such as a gas
pump or pinball machine and people have to
guess what you are) - these and any other
children's games that call on the imagination are excellent. They loosen you up, get
you to have fun, pique the child in you.
Particularly good for actors who are rigid
and afraid to be silly.

39. Believability

This exercise is far more than an Imagination
Preparation. In fact, its roots are entwined

in the very nucleus of what acting is. I've
often thought that any one branch of our large
tree of craft could in itself be developed into a total approach to acting. Music as a
choice and all the endless selections you
could use might become an entire system of
work. Getting a physical sense of animals
or of different people or inanimate objects
could be enlarged and used exclusively as
your approach. Believability is that kind of
branch. It is that important. But why put
all your weight on one branch, when together
they give you a more solid foundation, a more
varied choice of tools toward dimensional
acting?

When children pretend and play their games,
they believe because they want to believe and
so their wooden crate is a jet airplane. But
often when an actor gets up on stage, he chal-
lenges his belief. He says to himself, "Well,
this could never happen to me. This is really
hard to believe. I'd never behave like that."
instead of starting where children start.

I began the Believability as a Round Exercise,
hoping that if the actors in my class repeated
it weekly, they would heighten and expand their
willingness to believe. If repeatedly the actor wants to believe, as children do, and
chooses to believe in imaginary events and
takes these events personally, then his willingness to believe will grow. Believing becomes a habit.

JELLYBEAN: IT TAKES MORE ENERGY
TO NEGATE BELIEF THAN IT DOES TO BELIEVE

After a couple of months of doing the Believability Round every week, I was aware of some
significant things beginning to happen. People visiting the class during a Believability

230

would often get very embarrassed and walk
out, phoning me later to apologize and explain that they felt they didn't have a
right to be there that night, when everybody was being so personal. They felt like
Peeping Toms, spying on the privacies of
other people. I realized that they didn't
understand it was an exercise. They believed every minute of it! What a marvelous
audience response to a theatrical event!

An author wrote a book after visiting the
class and in the book called me all kinds of
terrible things, because he believed the
Believability exercise, misinterpreted the
purpose of it and took as true everything
that was totally untrue. The actors themselves would often get so involved in the
Believability, they'd be affected long after
the exercose was over. It's not unusual for
an actor to storm out of class during this
Round, upset by something which he knows is
untrue, but his belief has become stronger
than his knowledge.

I realized that the energy of the group feeds
each actor's willingness to believe. One
person's belief stimulates another's. Twenty
people feeding the imaginary circumstances
eliminates that line between hypothetical
and real until the air is charged with excitement. Both actors and audience reach a
point where they cannot separate the truth
from the untruth. Belief and disbelief get
confused in a mesh of possible truths. Pretty soon you find yourself believing everything. The point is that a good Believability exercise is good theatre. The actors
are unpredictable and extremely exciting to
watch. There is reality in everything that's
happening and that's what acting sould always
be.

But I saw that actors who were capable of total belief in this exercise were still having difficulty creating realities in their scene work. If you sit in a Believability Round and you're exciting and affectable and unpredictable and then you get up on a stage in a scene and you're not any of those things, it's because you haven't dealt with the obstacles between you and your belief. What you can do in a Round or in Two-People Believability you can also do in a scene, if you eliminate the obstacles to your willingness to believe and function in terms of that believed situation. Some of these obstacles are the obligation you feel to the material, your need to be "good", your need to feel a specific emotional response, emotional and intellectual concepts of all kinds, the value judgements you put on different emotions and so forth. Your choice to believe can overcome all these obstacles at once. Of course, you can shore up and support your Believability with other craft elements such as Sense Memory Choices (the greatest Believability exercise in the world is a Sense Memory exercise), use of Available Stimuli, Suggestions of all kinds, and so on. But if you start with Believability, you're half way down the road.

You're given a set of hypothetical circumstances - Hedda Gabler, for instance. You're not married to this man. This is not your home. This is a stage set. We're in Hollywood and not in Sweden and you're not fascinated by guns. As a matter of fact, you hate guns and have never owned one. Those are a set of circumstantial lies. So what you do through the craft is to substitute those lies with your own realities. But you've got to believe the existence of your own imaginary realities before you can function. The Believability exercise trains you to do that.

A Sense Memory Choice is a way to create your own reality on the stage. You can create a room that is personal to you other than the stage set, a room which makes you feel as much at home there as Hedda feels in her own house. Believability exists as a part of sensory process, because you must be able to believe that you see, hear, feel, taste and smell something which actually is not there. However, Believability also allows you to believe just by the decision to believe. You can hold the gun in your hand and simply choose to believe that this object can and will end your life. The success you have in sensorily creating your room will support your belief in the deadliness of the gun. This does not mean that you must first create a reality sensorily in order to stimulate your belief by a simple decision. You may just as simply believe you're in your own room. The craft processes are only designed to support your belief.

Start the Believability Exercise in a round, mixing truth with untruths. A person might say to another person, "I waited for you until ten o'clock this morning, Tom. You didn't answer your phone." And of course, it isn't true, but Tom is obligated to respond in some way and he might say, "What are you talking about? We didn't have a rehearsal this morning." And then the first person might reply, "You mean you forgot? You're always doing that, Tom. Why do you do that? Don't you care?" Or Tom's first response might be something like, "Well - you know, I hate to say this, but I overslept. I heard the phone ringing, and I knew it was you but I was afraid to answer because I was afraid you'd be mad at me, like you are now."

A Believability Exercise can start with a

total untruth directed at another person, such
as that one about the rehearsal. Or you can
start with something untrue about yourself, a
story you tell about yourself which the other
people get drawn into believing. For example,
you might say, "I feel very reluctant - uh -
I know this isn't a Reluctancy exercise - but
I'm reluctant to say this on my last night in
class. I'm going to New York in the morning
and - uh - boy, I hate to say anything because
I'm so excited inside I'm busting, but I got
a lead in a Broadway show." Then people con-
gratulate you. "That's fantastic!. . . What
play?. . . Who's the director?. . . I told you
that would happen if you'd just stick with it
. . . " Somebody else might burst into tears
and confess jealousy of your good fortune and
even admit she'd always hated you because you
always get the good things. Her explosion
might evoke chiding responses from some of
the people and others might confess that they
too had always been jealous of you.

Or you can start with a truth and gradually
weave into it some untruths. "You know, when
you and I had coffee last week after class
and we got into that big, heavy talk, I
thought about it all week." Now you may
actually have had coffee with that person
last week, and you may have gotten into a
big discussion, but now you can take that
truth into an entirely fictitious area. You
use the truth as a springboard and then people can bandwagon and either challenge or
supplement the elements of what you're talking about. Someone might say, "I don't believe that. I don't believe a word you're
saying." And instead of this criticism
stopping the flow of the exercise, it can
be used as part of the Believability. You
can answer, "That's what's wrong with you,
Jean. You never believe anything." And the

others can bandwagon and support your accusation.

All the people in the round can jump in and build something that one person starts. Or if one person is encountering another, people can take sides or start a one-to-one conflict with that person, saying something like, "Hey, I've noticed that about you, Joe. You do things like that. What she said about you is true. You've been like that with me." And that could either be true, semi-true or not true at all. The exercise builds and grows in momentum of belief.

There's a certain trap to avoid in the Believability Round. The exercise has a tendency to get conflict-ridden, negative and hostile, mainly because in encountering another person, people choose areas of conflict which are often negative in order to get something going and to elicit an immediate response from another person. That's a trap, leading to an overload of negativity in the group. It is not only depressing but can sometimes take the place of more tender and vulnerable areas, areas which are really harder to expose because they're often more frightening. To avoid this trap, encourage yourself to bring in as many positives as negatives. "Joan, I love you. I've always loved you. It's hard for me to admit that to you, but I really love you." And then Joan might reply, "I've often felt that from you, but it embarrasses me and I don't know how to handle it." Now that positive exchange can be partially true or not true at all, and that positivity can build on another and another.

The dialogues may either run themselves out to a conclusion or some other person may

start a whole new thing in the middle. For
example, the dialogue about the rehearsal. . .
"Tom, you didn't show up for rehearsal this
morning. You didn't answer your phone." And
Tom says, "I'm sorry, I overslept," etc. Then
somebody else might say to someone, "You know
that coat you bought for me? It was stolen
out of my apartment." Of course, these statements come one at a time, because if everybody
talks at once, it's mayhem. But various dialogues can interweave. The two people who
started with the rehearsal argument may go
back to it later in the exercise and take it
further into deeper, more personal areas.
There is no clear-cut form. You may bandwagon on a dialogue or disregard it and start
your own.

John Fiorito begins a Believability with Flo.
"Flo, last night when I was over at your house
for dinner, I was hurt by you. You hurt my
feelings. You were cold and detached and un-
communicative. And when I got home it was
hard to go to sleep, because I really felt
hurt." Flo might say, "I'm sorry, John. It
wasn't intentional. I had a bad week." John
might continue with, "I think you do that a
lot with me. I think you take advantage of
the fact that you know how I feel about you.
You use it. You manipulate me and I think
you get something out of it." Flo might come
back with, "John, are you going to start that
paranoid crap with me? I don't take advantage of anything. I just had a bad week, a
bad month, a bad year, John."

Now John may not have been there for dinner
last night or ever, but he may have chosen to
start the Believability with Flo because he
has, in truth, a real attraction to her which
is not returned. He chooses to work in an
area which has its seeds in a personal truth.

By the same token, Flo might really have had
"a bad day, a bad month, a bad year," as she
says to John. She may actually, at this
moment, be filled with despair about her
life. In this instance, the facts aren't
true, but the feelings are.

Instead of just sitting and listening to Flo
and John, which you're allowed to do if you
want, you might jump in and say, "Yeah, John,
you have a tendency to get hurt very easily.
You imagine hurts that aren't there. Last
week when I walked into class and you said
I didn't say hello to you, it's because I
didn't see you, John, and that's the truth."
Then John might defend himself and say, "You
walked right by me. You looked at me and
snubbed me, man. Don't give me any of that
crap, bacause you did." Then he might go on
with Flo.

Sometimes,after starting a Believability
exercise, you forget that it's an exercise.
One night in the round David said he wanted
to share something with the class. He said
that he and Leigh, a girl in the class, were
engaged to be married. Everyone was sur-
prised and elated. "Gee, how long has this
been going on?. . . That's wonderful!. . .
etc., etc. He explained they'd kept it a
secret because they didn't want everyone
talking about it before they'd made their
decision. People congratulated them and I
thought to myself, "Gee, that's really nice,
they'll make a nice couple." Leigh was glow-
ing. She blushed and there were tears in her
eyes as she talked about their future together.
A week later I was sitting out by my pool taking some sun and I got this warm glow, a feeling for David and Leigh. I thought, "Gee,
isn't that nice how people meet in my class
and some of them get married."

I felt personally responsible for the match
and I got very involved in this good feeling
about it and then suddenly I realized it happened in a Believability exercise. It wasn't
true. It never was true. And it isn't true
now. I felt I'd been had. But it proved to
me my desire to believe was so strong that
even though I knew somewhere it wasn't true,
the seed of belief grew and lived a whole
week.

As you participate in a Believability round
over a period of time, keep pushing your line
of believability further and further away by
gradually making things harder and harder to
believe. Be aware when something is impossible for you to believe and try to find out
why. If you can define what makes you doubt
your belief, then maybe there's a way you can
deal with that, some adjustment you can make
that helps you to believe. Ask yourself what
seed of truth exists that could hook you into
the lie. Next time when this same kind of
untruth comes up, you'll be more ready to believe it and able to make the adjustment on
your feet rather than after the fact. Limits
of believability vary from actor to actor.
Get to know your own personal limits and keep
stretching them. Keep lowering your Thresh-
hold of Believability. *As you become more
able to believe in anything, you become more
able to believe in everything.*

Believability exercises - the Round, Two-Peop
and One-Person - are great for your imaginati
since the imagination is constantly called up
in these exercises. You can also use Believa
bility as a choice in a scene by simply choos
to believe that this is a room out of your li
this woman is your mother, that suitcase is
really full of ransom money. Or you can use
Believability to supplement another choice be
cause belief is implicit in the success of an

238

choice. Besides all these uses, Believability is a root training exercise that
must become part of your whole approach
to acting. The threads of it should run
through every exercise you do.

JELLYBEAN: IT IS AS EASY TO BELIEVE
AS IT IS TO DISBELIEVE

II. PREPARATIONS FOR RELATING TO PEOPLE, OBJECTS AND PLACES

In this section, as before, preparation means
preparing to act, to do a scene in a film or
a play. Getting related to the other actor
is very important, because most acting occurs
between two or more people. Getting related
to the place and the objects in it is also
important, because every time you act, what
you do and how you do it depends on where
you do it. The place and what it means to
you affects your character in the scene. The
writer purposely sets the action of a scene
in a particular place because that place has
something to do with what's going on and has
a specific influence on the people in the
scene. For example, I would behave differently having a domestic argument on the corner of Hollywood and Vine than I would in my
own bedroom. My voice would be different.
My relationship to the other person would be
distracted by passersby. My sense of privacy
would be distracted.

The following sequence begins with exercises
for getting related to the other actor, but
that doesn't mean you must start there before you work on the place and objects.
Start with whatever is necessary. In some
scenes the relationship between the two
characters may be far more significant than

239

their relation to the place. In an all-con-
suming love affair, for instance, the lovers
are more important to each other than any of
the places they're in. In this case, you
would prepare for your relationship to your
partner first and enrich it later by creating
the place. In other scenes it's the other
way around - the place is more important than
the actor's relationship, or equally so.

40. Two-People Believability

This is done the same way it is done in the
Believability round. Either person can start
or they can start simultaneously. The exercise can be used simply to heighten your willingness to believe or you can choose to lead
yourself into an area of believability which
parallels the circumstances of the material.

Excerpt from a class tape, January, 1973:

RUTH: She had me almost believing what I - I
       - but I knew what was in my locket!

JOAN: The line of believing that you speak of
       Eric, occurred for me at the very begin-
       ning, the very first lie I told I was
       aware of its being a lie and I took a
       deep breath and some little echo of the
       past said, "Oh now, Joanie, don't lie."
       You know, some little mother's gover-
       nessy voice. And I took a deep breath
       and said a very simple easy thing, a
       simple ordinary untruth and once I got
       over that hump, Eric, my believability
       increased and I got so bizarre. I got
       hold of this locket and I believed that
       there were baby's toenails in it.

ERIC: You mean, like it was an occult talis-
       man?

240

JOAN: I believed it! I believed that this witch - that she had a pressed embryo in there and. . .

RUTH: I <u>knew</u> that it had my husband's picture in there, but she made me feel really creepy about it.

ERIC: Joan's believability kicked off Ruth's believability that there was something strange and mystical about that locket when, in fact, Ruth, you feel very warm about that locket and knew all the time what was in it. But Joan made you doubt and feel differently about your locket. Therefore, the two of you, starting with an untruth, a lie, were able to create an emotional life together based on that lie which you chose to believe.

41. Blind Investigate

Two actors close their eyes and investigate each other with their four other senses. They touch each others' faces, arms, bodies. They smell, taste, listen. The purpose for this kind of investigation is to take much less for granted. Our eyes lead us to taking things for granted and when sight is denied, you become much more sensorily related and involved and in tune with the other person. From that point of involvement you are then much readier to work with your partner towards dealing with the material, because you are sensorily related.

42. Observe, Wonder and Perceive

Refer to Chapter II under <u>Two-People Observe, Wonder and Perceive</u>. This exercise definitely gets you related to the other actor. You can do it with or without the other actor knowing it.

43. Talk About What You're Most Afraid Of

Two actors talk to each other, expressing moment-to-moment their fears in relation to eac[
other.

MICHELLE: I'm afraid to say the first line.

CHARLES : Me Too. I'm glad you have the fir[
           line. And I'm afraid you don't li[
           me.

MICHELLE: That's nonsense, Charles. I don't
           dislike you at all. I like you.

CHARLES : I'm afraid of this material. I
           don't think I can do it.

MICHELLE: It scares me too. And I'm afraid
           of you, because you've had much
           more experience than I've had.

CHARLES : Maybe so, but I'm afraid to be her[
           because I'm afraid of what will or
           won't happen. . . etc.

The expression of fears between two people of
ten eliminates obstacles that would ordinaril[
plague the rehearsal process. Things that
fester, hidden away, keep you from your own
vulnerability.

44. Non-Verbal Communication

You relate to your partner without words. Yo[
may use sounds and gibberish and physical mov[
ments. Start by relating to what is going on
at the moment between the two of you. The ex[
cise encourages a communication which is not
dependent on the meaning and the understandin[
of words. It elicits more visceral, emotional
responses instead of a cerebral, verbal rappo[

242

45. Relate Moment-to-Moment With What You Feel

Two people relate to each other verbally and non-verbally in a stream-of-consciousness form, expressing moment-to-moment everything that's going on individually and between them. Include in your conversation all those thoughts and impulses that have nothing to do with the other person, such as sounds outside, your awareness of being here and looking for things to talk about, besides those impulses and feelings you have toward the other person. This preparation trains you to include everything so that you don't have to function in spite of anything, right from the very beginning of a two-people relationship.

46. Share

Share with each other those things which are personally meaningful to you. It can be about anything in any area. The purpose for sharing meaningful things is that it gets you closer to each other, more involved and caring. If, as people, you feel for each other, then, as actors, you start with that level of feeling and carry it into the material.

47. Two-People Trick

This preparation is used primarily as an antidote to premeditated acting, because it keeps both actors in a state where they don't know what's coming next. It can be done while they're saying the lines of the scene or while they're improvising on the scene or during a Believability or really any kind of communication exercise, verbal or non-verbal. They both can agree to do

it or one actor can decide to do it without
the other's knowledge or permission. Either
actor suddenly does or says something unex-
pectedly, often large or bizarre things,
sometimes conventional things, but always
unexpected. The other actor must respond
impulsively to how the trick affected him
and include his impulsive reaction in the
relationship.

For example, two people are calmly talking
together about what a nice day it is and
suddenly one of them jumps up and starts
screaming or doing an Abandonment exercise.
The other actor is obligated to respond to
however that truly makes him feel, whether
or not those feelings have any logical connection to what they were talking about. A
more subtle example might be in a love-scene,
when the two actors are exchanging passionate
lines and caresses. At any point one of the
actors might become cold and detached, with-
drawing from the partner while still mouthing
the passionate words of the material. The
other one then must deal with how that withdrawal really makes him feel, rather than
cling to his concept of the scene.

The purpose of the Two-People Trick is to encourage both actors to trust their impulses
in responding to each other. The more they
trust, the more impulsive their relationship
will be, not only within the exercise or the
improvisation, but also within the scene.
Actors commonly hold concepts about how a
scene should go or how a character would or
would not behave, and these concepts are usually restrictive and narrow. As a result,
the acting comes out smoothly, perhaps com-
petently, but conventionally. It's amazing
how the work takes on many surprisingly unique
and human colors when actors find out how many

different kinds of behavior fit into any given scene. Besides its use as a preparation for getting related to the other actor, the Trick exercise can be used in rehearsals and in performances to keep yourself from being predictable and premeditated.

48. Imaginary Monologue To A Real Partner But Talking To Someone Else

The instructions for Imaginary Monologue appear earlier in this chapter. In the exercise here you talk to the other actor, but the things you're saying are things you're saying to your father or wife or whomever you've chosen to talk to. In the usual Imaginary Monologue you're talking to someone who is not there. You're speaking to an empty chair. Now in this exercise the other actor exists and the fact that he's there and responding to what you're saying gives your Imaginary Monologue a very different dimension. You are provoking responses from the other actor which may or may not be similar to the behavior of your father or wife and this leads to an unpredictable relationship. The other actor and your imaginary person meld into one and hopefully takes you to the desired emotional life.

49. Imaginary Dialogue With Real Partner, Take Personally What's Said To You

Do this the same way you do the Imaginary Monologue To Real Partner, except in this exercise both actors are talking to imaginary people and you choose to take personally whatever the other actor says to you. The value of it is that both people are responding to real and imaginary stimuli at the same time. There are elements of

Believability and also elements of the Trick
exercise, because it's impossible for the
other actor to behave as your imagined person would and you have to deal with these
constant surprises in his behavior. It makes
for a very exciting two-people preparation.

50. Pick Up On Everything You Didn't Notice Before

You can use this exercise either for getting
related to the other actor or for getting
related to the place and objects. As the
name suggests, you decide to notice all
those things about the person or the place
that you never noticed before. What color
are her eyes? How long is her neck? You
may never have observed how tall she is.
How many windows in this room? What things
are hanging on the walls?

51. Make Yourself Comfortable In This Place

You've come into a strange place, a rehearsal
room, the stage at a first rehearsal, an office waiting room. Begin by asking yourself
How can I make myself comfortable in this
place? You might choose to do the exercise
by becoming involved in what really exists,
first acknowledging your discomfort and then
observing and perceiving the objects in the
room, which gets you out of yourself and
related to the place. Another way is to
use the sense memory process to create
familiar objects around which, if they
really were in this place, would make you
feel comfortable and secure.

52. Build A Beautiful Place Around You

This is a sense memory exercise, which you
use to build a place that is more creatively

stimulating than the place you're in. For instance, you can change a drab sound stage into a beautiful Hawaiian beach or to a forested mountain-top.

53. Sensory Speculation

The exercise has several purposes. It's a sense memory practice, an additional sensitizing exercise and a way to get you more related to the place you're in and to the person you're working with. You ask speculative questions. What would it feel like to touch that wall over there? What would the texture feel like on the tips of my fingers? You're asking these questions from a distance away and you respond in your fingertips to what you sensorily imagine. Then you walk over to the wall and feel it, finding out how close your speculation was to the real wall on your fingertips. What would that ashtray smell like? Try to imagine in your nose the component parts of that odor. Maybe you see that there are old butts and gum wrappers in the ashtray. Sensorily speculate on all those elements and then walk over and relate to the real object. Choose objects that engage all five senses. Give your senses a real workout. You can do Sensory Speculation with a person too.

54. Affecting How You Already Feel

This is one of the most important areas of preparation. In order to get to where you want to go in a scene, you have to know where you are now. Let's say you've done all your preparations for getting ready to act. You've done your Relaxation exercises, your Sensitizing and Personal Inventories and now you're ready, but you want to feel something other than what you're feeling now, because you know that's the obligation in the material. Often this intermediate step is overlooked.

The actor jumps from a general preparedness to a specific obligation without building a bridge in between. Even the most seasoned actor can fall into this chasm. He feels good, he's ready to act and he starts to work for his choice in the scene. But that choice he's working for may be very hard to come to because of the way he's feeling. He's excited and turned on to acting and creative, but the person he's playing in the scene is very shy, tender and vulnerable. It's difficult to go from excitement to shyness without some interim steps. When he tries to make this jump, he's often disappointed that his choice doesn't work as well as he expected. He says, "Last night in the theatre I used this choice and it took me on a trip. It was wonderful! Tonight I went on stage and worked for the same choice and - nothing. Nothing happened." Some actors are totally confused by that. They feel the choice is no good anymore and they discard it.

But it's not the choice. The way he felt last night was very conducive to his being affected by that choice. And the way he is feeling tonight is subtly different, but different enough so that he is not as easily affected by that same choice. He's a little more insulated tonight and protective. He had an argument with someone and the echoes of it are still rumbling around inside on a less than conscious level. On the surface he's not aware of a great difference between last night and tonight, but because he did not do his Personal Inventories and find out how he really feels, he can't relate to the

differences. And those subtle things are
enough to keep his choices from working.

If he did a Personal Inventory, maybe he'd
find out that he has residual resentments
from that argument and these unexpurgated
emotions are preventing him from being affected by his choice. Once he identifies
his obstacles through Personal Inventory,
then his course is clear. He must choose
an interim preparation to expurgate those
residual feelings. He might do a Vesuvius
or have an Imaginary Monologue with the
person saying all the things he couldn't
say this afternoon, or an Abandonment or
Dump or any number of large expressive
exercises, thereby freeing himself of those
trapped impulses that keep him from functioning. But before he can do any kind of
interim preparation, he must first know
what's going on inside.

After doing your general preparations, find
out how you feel. Then you might try your
choice as a way of taking your emotional
temperature. If the choice works, you're
ready. If it doesn't, go back to your Personal Inventory and locate the obstacles.
You might need some kind of interim bridge.
Affecting how you already feel is a very
important part of preparing, not only because it changes what is to what you want
in the scene, but also because it enables
you to repeat your work.

After finding out *how you feel* through Personal Inventory or any number of other exercises (sometimes you're so insulated that
Personal Inventory doesn't reveal much to
you and you have to get into larger, more
freeing exercises), then find out *how you
want to feel* by *identifying the obligation*
in the material. The obligation is that

emotional life that you want to experience.
What do you want to feel about the other
person in the scene? What do you want to
feel about the place? What does your character feel generally, conglomeratively.
There are thematic obligations, time obligations and many other kinds, but most often your first concern is your relationship
to the other person. Find out specifically
how you want to feel in that relationship
and then find out where you are in your
present moment-to-moment life. Then you
will have some ideas about what you can do
to go from one State of BEING to another.

55. Affecting The Way You Feel About The Other Actor

1. How do I feel about him (her) here and now?

2. How do I want to feel about him (her) in the scene?

3. What Availabilities can I use?

4. Isolate and emphasize the Availabilities.

5. Endowment - a sensory choice.

This series of questions is a preparation I
found as an actor and in helping other actors.
You can use it under fire and on your feet.
It really works. It's a list of things you
ask yourself in a beginning rehearsal when
you start a scene. First you ask yourself,
"How do I feel about that actor (actress)?
How do I feel about her right here and now?"
Take a kind of Personal Inventory about what
you see, hear, taste, smell and feel in relation to that particular actress. You might
say to yourself, "Well, she's all right. She
doesn't thrill me to death. She's an

interesting looking girl. She's got pretty
hair. Pretty eyes. I like her. I don't
dislike her. I don't feel any strong, important emotional feelings about her. I
feel kind of a neutral feeling. I guess
if I got to know her, I might feel other
things. I don't know anything about her.
She's kind of bland, actually. . . etc."

Once you've taken that kind of inventory
and really know how you feel about her,
then ask yourself, "How do I want to feel
about her in the scene?" You've read the
scene and you understand what the author
wants and you identify your obligation.
In this case, maybe the author wants you
to feel extremely excited about the girl,
sparks flying between you, an electricity
about this woman that attracts you power-
fully on every level, sexual, emotional,
intellectual. That's a very different
state than what you feel about her now.

The third step you take, after you've found
out how you feel and defined how you want to
feel and discovered that they're poles apart,
is to ask yourself the question, "What is
available? What is there existing in this
actress that I can use to stimulate the feelings I want?" You really look the person
over from head to toe, not just visually,
but using all your senses to explore all
the Availibilities that might appeal to you.
A sound in her voice, a scent, an odor, the
shape of her breasts, the way she moves,
something you see behind her eyes, what her
hair and skin feel like, how she clasps your
hand. Once you've found several things which
are there, several Availabilities, then the
next step is to isolate those elements one
at a time and emphasize your relationship to
each one. For instance, maybe her mouth
reminds you of someone you were once in love

251

with and looking at her mouth rekindles unconscious responses to a love affair you had
five years ago. One at a time emphasize your
relationship to each Availability by not only
looking at it, but relating to it with all
your senses, asking yourself questions, smelling, listening, touching. Emphasis does not
mean exclusion of the total person. While
you are using the one Availability, you continue to relate to the total person. You
hope that the Availabilities will take you
to where you want to go, but even if they
don't, they will start you in the right direction. They will start you off in the
area of excitement and attraction.

After you've exhausted all that is available
(in some cases that will be enough) and you
find yourself closer to how you want to feel
about her, but still no sparks, then you must
go on to the next step, which is Endowment.
Endowment is a sensory process. You create
sensory elements related to an object, in
this instance, a person. You endow your
partner with physical attributes, emotional
attributes, vocal behavior and intellectual
attitudes that appeal to you, things which
you know if they really existed in this actress would excite you. You might create a
look in her eyes, endow her with intelligence
that manifests itself in some sensory way,
bathe her in exotic scents, give her longer
eyelashes. You can work to create her naked
and endow her with exciting sexual odors.
Whatever you choose to endow her with, you
do it through the sense memory process. It
is not done through suggestion.

56. Preparational Inventories

What kind of preparations do I need? This is
a question you ask yourself repeatedly. Starting from your general preparations, which

includes your Personal Inventory, and on
through your identification of the demands
in the material and the changes you make in
how you feel about the other actor, you are
constantly taking Preparational Inventories.
What kind of preparations do I need to take
me where I want to go?

Preparational Inventory is similar to Personal Inventory, except that it focuses much
more specifically on your feelings as they
relate to the obligation and on your knowledge
of what kinds of preparations are available
to you and how they work for you. Your growing experience is important here. Having
worked with many preparations, many kinds of
choices, your experience will give you the
ability to know what they did for you. Gradually you will catalogue your personal repertoire of preparational choices.

57. Create A Different Environment

Where you are has a great deal to do with the
way you behave. Changing your environment
will change how you feel. You can create a
different environment through several ways:
sense memory, isolation and emphasis, endowment, suggestion, pretending, bringing with
you real objects that are personally meaningful. You're in a park and there's a lot
of litter around you and it's a drab day and
you want to be filled with the joy of nature
and life. Through isolation and emphasis
you can use that beautiful tree in front of
you, relating only to the tree and to the
green patch of grass beneath it. Hopefully
you will stimulate a sense of being close
to nature in a joyous environment. Or you
can endow the tree with more foliage than it
has, birds, sweet-smelling blossoms and put
a blue sky behind it with billowing white
clouds.

58. Sensory Choice To Meet Obligation

You can choose to work for an object which is
not really here. Object, of course, means
anything inanimate, animate, a person, a sound,
a piece of music, a photograph, a texture, part
of a place, a letter, an odor - anything that
once created sensorily, will affect you the way
you want to be affected.

59. Make Everything Around You More Important
Than You

You choose to make everything around you more
important to you than you. You can fulfill
the choice through a simple involvement by
asking questions that aren't necessarily sensory. Where did that piece of furniture come
from? I wonder who it belongs to and what
period it is. Is it an original or a copy?

Or you can ask what-if questions, sensorily
speculating about the things around you. Or
through the sensory process you can modify
the objects, giving them different colors,
textures, shapes, creating a person in the
chair, anything that makes the place more
interesting. You can Pretend, Story-Tell,
Fantasize, any approach to get you more involved in your surroundings and absorbed by
them. This preparation changes your emotional life by getting you out of yourself,
relating to a place outside of your own concerns.

60. Say Words To Yourself Relating To A
Meaningful Experience

This is another way to change how you feel.
The experience can be real or imaginary as
long as it is meaningful and has impact on
you. Don't tell yourself a story, because
that will lead you to report rather than

experience. Say single words, or short
phrases while re-experiencing the event.

III. <u>PREPARATIONS FOR DOING THE ROLE</u>

Even though a preparation can be as complex
as any of the work you do to fulfill the
scene, preparation for doing the scene does
not mean execution of the scene. It means
getting ready to tackle the scenic obligations, understanding them and making them
clear to yourself. Preparations are to
prepare you for the selection and usage of
choices. The more courageous your preparations are, the greater the risk of failure,
but the richer your work will be at those
times when you're successful. Remember, you
use preparation not only to fulfill the emotional life of the material, but also to get
to BEING. You can't run the race without
getting ready to run.

<u>From Joan's Journal:</u> <u>Using Preparation On</u>
                        <u>The Job</u>

"I arrived at Columbia Ranch having had two
hours sleep last night. We shot the love
scene today. It was 100 degrees in the
studio. I knew with heat and lack of sleep
I'd have to use my craft skillfully to get
through the work. By the end of the day I
realized I'd never been quite as successful
as I was today in consciously employing
things to help myself.

The preparations I chose were not done paren-
thetically. That is, I didn't go off behind
a flat to work and I didn't appear to anyone
around as if I were <u>doing</u> anything special.
Instead I found ways to weave the exercises
into the life on the set, encountering and

relating to the people in various ways and responding to their reactions. This is a big improvement for me, because I used to keep myself isolated, cloistered in my dressing room and then I'd have to cross that Big Line between the privacy of my room and getting in front of the camera to do the scene. Today I found how to mix it all together.

The scene required me to be sensually alive and excited, really turned on to Rick. I sat in my chair while they set up the shot and did Tense and Relax, Logey, Sensitize and Personal Inventory. Found out I'm feeling depressed and anxious. A friend of mine got arrested last night and went to jail on false charges. I had to go downtown around midnight and help raise bail and get her out of Sybil Brand. Terrible place. So I did some Ego Exercises and Positivity to bring myself up and brighten my outlook. After I felt better I did Sensuality to get myself in touch with my body. Feeling numb, not sexy at all. Ten or fifteen minutes of Sensuality got the juices going. We did the master shot and Rick's close-ups and then it was lunch time.

After lunch I went into a slump. Oppressively hot, maybe 105 degrees by now. My scalp was so wet that the hairdresser could hardly move the hair without the whole shape falling down. She did her best and then I moved to the make-up chair, but the old nanny goat refused to touch me up, because he said the director would yell at him if I was late on the set. I felt deprived. I felt I needed the touch of hands on my face to get me through the afternoon. I chose to do a Reluctancy at that point, telling the guy how unpleasant he was to work with, how

256

unprofessional, etc. He did the touch-up.
I went on the set, shaking, but expurgated
and felt a lot better. Had I not done that,
it would have boiled inside me, the Per-
petual Nice Girl, and it would have kept
me from being able to act. I was trembling
from the risk I'd taken, so I did a quick
Self Perspective, recalling myself five
years ago, a scared and silent mouse on
the set, as compared to now, asking for
what is due to me. This calmed me, but I
still wasn't where I'd been before lunch.
So I did a Silly Dilly, bursting into opera-
tic song and running around squaking like a
chicken. Everybody laughed and that picked
up my spirits.

When it came time for my close-up, I prepared by doing an Imaginary Monologue to
Larry, a gorgeous man I'd just met last
Sunday. I had about half an hour to create
him there and I asked to be my own stand-in
so that I could work in the set. I used
sense memory to create Larry. He was standing there under the lights, languid and
seductive. I talked to him semi-audibly
and he talked back to me, making me laugh
and giggle and blush, which is just the behavior I wanted in the scene. I moved him
over to the sofa. He sat down and crossed
his long legs, winked at me suggestively.
By the time they were ready to shoot I was
ready to work. I did it in one take and
the director was hugging me afterwards and
the cameraman said I came across very sexy
on camera. Self Perspective again - remember five years ago? - not sexy at all, very
cold and uptight on camera."

These are the preparations that Joan chose
to use to meet the emotional obligations of
this particular scene in this show. The
preparational exercises you can choose from

are numerous and the combinations are endless.
You select your own cluster of preparations
not only to fulfill the demands of the material, but also to deal with the circumstances
surrounding the execution of that day's work,
which includes the weather - 105 degrees, how
you feel - two hours sleep, the way the director relates to you - or the make-up man, your
physical state of health, your mental outlook.
The circumstances around you influence your
State of BEING and dictate the nature and mixture of your preparational choices. The obligations of the material remain constant, but
your State of BEING is ever-changing.

Some suggested preparations:

61. Two-People Three Part Relationship

1. Wonder, Perceive and Observe.

2. Work for a sensory choice without any emo-
    tional obligation.

3. Obligate yourself to an emotional result
    and work for a sensory choice.

62. Two-People Preparation

1. Investigate each other in all ways, ver-
    bally and sensorily.

2. Go with what is, expressing moment-to-
    moment, verbally and non-verbally, every-
    thing you feel.

3. Isolate and emphasize many parts of the
    person and see how each isolation makes
    you feel.

4. Work for any sensory choice in relation
    to the other person.

5. Obligate yourself to something you want to feel in relation to the person, make a choice and work for it.

This preparation helps you be ready to work with that specific actor. It may also facilitate the obligations of the text.

63. Group Preparation

A good workout for a rehearsal group or a class.

1. Wonder to yourself about everything in the room.

2. Wonder semi-audibly about one person.

3. Semi-audibly or out loud ask one question about each person you're curious about.

4. Two-People Wonder, Perceive and Observe. (Now the group is working in pairs and the director or teacher may decide to switch the pairs around during the following steps or keep them together.

5. Two-People Double Exposure.

6. Two-People Fun-Love-Trick.

7. Two-People Believability.

8. Two-People Sense Memory, working with and without the real object.

64. Pretend Series

1. Pretend by yourself. Keep it colorful and child-like.

2.   Pretend with another person.

3.   Pretend Sense Memory by yourself, combining Pretend with the Sense Memory process.

4.   Pretend Sense Memory with another person.

65.   Character Background Preparation

Good for a class or a rehearsal group or for two actors working on a scene together.

1.   Each one talks in the first person about his character in the play and the others ask questions, encouraging him to fill in the gaps.

2.   Each actor then works alone, sensorily creating, one at a time, the realities tha lead to the fulfillment of the character. For example, your character in the play talks a lot about his physical exhaustion. You may now work to create that exhaustion

3.   Each actor chooses a scene from the play, defines an emotional obligation in that scene and works for a choice.

66.   Three-Step Monologue

A preparation you do alone with a piece of dramatic material.

1.   Say the text of the monologue out loud, letting the words come out of the moment-to-moment life that is going on in you.

2.   Work for a choice not related to the emotional obligations in the monologue and say the text.

3.   Work for a choice that hopefully fulfills an obligation in the monologue, and say

the text. This preparation enables you
to sneak up on a choice while training
you to let the material come out of your
BEING.

<u>67. Four-Part Word Preparation</u>

1. Say words to yourself that affect you -
    meaningful words out of your life but
    not necessarily related to a single
    experience.

2. Define how you want to feel and say words
    that you think will make you feel that
    way.

3. Pick an experience, not knowing how the
    experience will affect you, and say words
    related to it.

4. Two people working on a scene - say the
    lines to each other and say your own af-
    fecting words in between the lines.

These groups are not sacred. You can mix
them up, borrow something from one, delete
something else, add any of the exercises in
this book and invent your own. What's really important is having your finger on your
pulse, knowing whether or not you need an
instrumental preparation at the moment or
if you need a preparation dealing with your
environment or with the other actor, or
whatever. This kind of intimate knowledge
about your instrument comes out of daily
practice, taking personal inventories, sensory inventories, doing all of those preparational exercises over a period of time
so that you are aware of what works and what
doesn't, and when. Failure and success are
an integral part of your never-ending growth
process. As you catalogue all those things
you find out about yourself related to

preparation, getting ready to act and, in fact
acting, you begin to get in touch with what
touches you.

BEING is not just a way of working, it is a
complete philosophy and a way of life. To
have the luxury of being able to do what you
want to do with your life, to experience who
you are and what you want, to pursue your
work for the sake of your own personal fulfillment and to reap the rewards of the creative process, this is what BEING affords. If
you use the exercises in this book and make
them a part of your life, and they become the
fabric of your behavior, you will embark on a
journey that leads to a never-neverland of
wonderfully full living experiences. The
work not only enriches your life enormously,
it allows you to act on a level that is unique
and rare in the theatre. You, the artist,
will develop the totality of your own individual statement.

"TO BE OR NOT TO BE, THAT IS THE QUESTION"

. . . . . AND THE ANSWER.

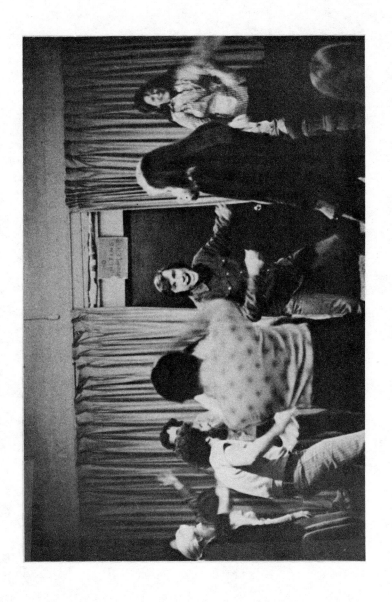

Students doing a "Large Positivity Exercise" in class

NOTES

NOTES

NOTES

NOTES